Adventures in Politics

Adventures in Politics

WE GO TO THE LEGISLATURE

BY

Richard L. Neuberger

New York

OXFORD UNIVERSITY PRESS

1954

For my sister

JANE

PREFACE

STATE GOVERNMENT has never before been so important as right now—today, tomorrow, and the next day. President Eisenhower has proposed that many of the vast responsibilities undertaken by the Federal government be turned back to the states. This dispersal of authority involves not only so-called New Deal measures but even some Federal functions which started half a century ago, when Theodore Roosevelt sat in the White House.

Already, the present administration has vested in a few states title to the rich oil reserves off the coasts of Texas, Louisiana, Florida, and California. The President has spoken of giving 'our public lands and forests' to a partnership of states. Social security, government housing, timber reserves, hydroelectric power projects, reclamation systems, employment and labor services—these are only a few of the activities President Eisenhower hopes to see shifted in some measure from Federal to state control.

The Department of the Interior has indicated that states and local communities should develop such rivers as the Columbia and Missouri, or else strategic dam sites will be transferred to private utility companies.

As the Federal government abdicates its role in many important realms, are the states ready to take over? The question becomes particularly pertinent when we remember that some of these realms of responsibility have been national in scope ever since their beginning.

Can state government now do the job? Is 'states' rights' a political slogan or a practical reality? Is it a platform to stand on or merely to run on? How these questions are answered may decide the fate of the Eisenhower administration. Far more significant, the result also may decide the future security of America in terms of the natural resources necessary to keep our nation strong and free.

Against a background of the personal experiences of my wife and myself in state government, I have written this little book. We have not been important personages—far from it. But we have had ringside seats in the arena where the President plans to locate the increased concentration of basic functions of government.

We have been members of a State Legislature in a historic and picturesque state of the Union, and it is in the legislatures where the fundamental policies of state government are shaped.

In 1940 my first term in the Oregon House of Representatives began. It ended before its natural expiration when I resigned to go into the Army, in June of 1942. After returning from service, I was defeated for the State Senate in the 'meat shortage' election of 1946. The margin of that defeat was 64,988 to 61,259. I still recall it vividly because it showed me that a local candidate often can be flotsam and jetsam when the currents are going against his party nationally.

In 1948 the voters elected me to the State Senate. I was re-elected in 1952. My wife was elected to the House of Representatives in 1950. The voters returned her in 1952. Her election was the best thing that ever happened to me. It put our best foot forward in the capitol at Salem. During the 1953 session of the Legislature the two of us constituted, between us, 15 per cent of the entire Democratic membership.

Portions of this book have appeared in the *Saturday Evening Post, Collier's, Reader's Digest, Harper's, The New York Times Magazine, Coronet, This Week, Redbook, American, Progressive, New Republic, Denver Post Empire Magazine, Frontier,* and *Butcher Workman.* I am grateful to the editors of these publications for permission to reprint this material.

I should be lacking in appreciation if I did not mention certain teachers of political science whose knowledge and counsel have helped me both as a legislator and as a journalist. I refer particularly to Maure Goldschmidt of Reed College, Peter H. Odegard of University of California, James D. Barnett and Waldo Schumacher of University of Oregon, Boyd A. Martin of University of Idaho, William A. McClenaghan of Oregon State College, and the late Father John B. Delaunay of Portland University. They are not responsible for the conclusions and advocacies of this book. Any errors, prejudices, or faults are mine alone.

My gratitude also extends to the three newspapermen who taught me all that I know about writing—Palmer Hoyt, L. H. Gregory, and the late Paul R. Kelty. That

these lifelong Republicans should have patiently
showed a Democrat how to grapple with the English
language is proof that we are not as rifted by partisanship as some would have us believe.

I doubt if a person can write with understanding
about the nation unless he knows thoroughly his own
particular realm within the nation. I want to express
my gratitude to those who have told me most about
Oregon and its people, resources, and history—Ralph
and Mabel Fenton, Ray Conway, Kelley Loe, William
O. Douglas, Cornelia Marvin Pierce, Mabel Southworth,
Joseph D. Sternberg, W. S. U'Ren, Edward M. Miller,
Albert Slaughter, and Jack Horton. These men and
women include a forest ranger, a Supreme Court Justice,
a chiropractor, and a member of the Council of the
American Medical Association.

Nor can I conclude this preface without thanking the
selfless researchers of the Public Library of Portland
and of the Oregon State Library for helping me to ad-
here as much as possible to accuracy and the hard granite of facts.

I also must thank my wife for being a restraining influence. She has persisted in reminding me that, occasionally, 'the other fellow may be right.' And who is to
doubt this in a sphere so full of uncertainties and
human frailties as the sphere of self-government?

That we as a nation do as well as we do, both at the
state and national level, must be taken as a hopeful sign
that the Almighty wishes us no harm.

R. L. N.

Portland, Oregon
June 1954

CONTENTS

xi

ADVENTURES IN POLITICS

– 1 –

WHAT'S REALLY WRONG

WITH STATE GOVERNMENTS?

I

STATE government in America has fallen upon sorry days when a substantial body of public opinion regards any natural resources entrusted to the care of the states as practically gone forever. Opponents of the Eisenhower administration use the opprobrious term 'giveaway' on the assumption that state governments lack both the will and the capacity to hold the people's heritage in escrow for the next generation.

When the tideland petroleum deposits were bestowed upon the governments of Texas, Louisiana, Florida, and California, more than thirty United States Senators contended this was tantamount to outright delivery to the oil companies—a claim that may not have been entirely lacking in prophecy. Many of these same Senators warn that proposed interstate compacts dealing with rivers will herald an end to hydroelectric development free of control by private utility interests. And the obvious alarm among campers, sports fishermen, and

3

botanists over possible transfer of areas in the national forests to the eleven Western states can mean only one thing. These people who revel in the outdoors fear destruction of every last tree and blade of grass by sawmills and livestock operators, if state governments should replace the Federal government as custodian of our woodland reserves.

Indeed, even some of the men who orate the most frequently and fervently on 'states' rights' have revealed, by their own actions, an absence of genuine personal attachment to this realm of government in which the founders of the nation magnanimously lodged all authority not specifically granted to Congress.

In our comparatively brief experience in state government, my wife and I have been struck by the hypocrisy of many who invoke the shibboleth of 'states' rights.' To begin with, they seem to have no genuine confidence that the states actually can do the job better than the Federal government. Secretary of the Interior McKay suggests that water resources should be 'given back' to the states, but what state has yet generated a single kilowatt on a stream of the magnitude of the Tennessee or the Columbia?

Furthermore, the loudest devotees of 'states' rights' often act more anxious than anyone else to get on the Federal payroll. Douglas McKay made haste to resign the governorship of Oregon so that he might enter the President's cabinet.

Although Lincoln declared that 'the Governors of the Northern states are the North,' there are few ambitious citizens today who would prefer a governorship to a seat in the United States Senate. This is demonstrated by the fact that nearly a third of the present

Senate consists of erstwhile Governors. The old, ginger-bread state executive mansions have been only halfway-houses on the road to Washington for these twenty-eight men, who blithely deserted state duties to serve the Federal colossus. And they number in their ranks such lusty verbal champions of state supremacy as Bricker of Ohio, Bridges of New Hampshire, Martin of Pennsylvania, Byrd of Virginia, Hickenlooper of Iowa, and Russell of Georgia.

What has happened? The governorship was once a political climax. On many dramatic occasions the Governor was invested with the power of life and death. Monarch of all he surveyed, the Governor could command a vast horde of state employees, few of them fettered by civil service. Furthermore, he was constantly titillated by knowledge of Governors of the recent past who had gone all the way, such as Woodrow Wilson of New Jersey, Calvin Coolidge of Massachusetts, and Franklin D. Roosevelt of New York.

But state government has not been up to the triple challenge of the great depression, global war, and rocketing inflation. The problems created by these events have been far beyond its scope. Anchored though the Federal government may be by tradition and checks and balances, it has the agility of a ballet troupe contrasted with the forty-eight states.

A lawyer who aspires to be Attorney General of Idaho must, if he is resolutely honest, gear himself to a salary of $5000 a year. In Arizona the chief law officer of the state is paid $6000 and in Missouri $7500. While a U. S. Senator from Oregon is allowed $39,540 annually to hire an office staff, the Governor of Oregon must handle infinitely more administrative responsibilities with a payroll of $28,296. Utah's Governor has ruled a state of 700,000 people for a wage of $7500, which is less than that paid to innumerable functionaries in Federal bureaus. And the pay for state legislators makes even these salaries seem of movie-star proportions by comparison. Few states compensate their lawmakers enough to pay for bacon and beans and blankets while bivouacked at the state capital, to say nothing of keeping the home-fires going.

Federal grants-in-aid have helped to make the states mere principalities of Washington, D. C. In 1931 the national government paid $219,162,574 into state treasuries to finance certain activities. Dominant among these modest undertakings were rural post roads, trunk highways, and the National Guard. By 1951 the total grants-in-aid had multiplied more than ten times, to $2,280,959,373. And the principal things which this money sustained were functions which, twenty years earlier, only reformers and agitators would have considered matters for Federal concern. Foremost were such items as old-age assistance, aid to dependent children and the blind, school lunches, unemployment compensation, and the planning and construction of public hospitals.

In 1931 road-building projects used up 71 per cent of all Federal financial grants to the states. Two decades later, social welfare programs took 68 per cent of an enormously expanded series of grants. Pressure by the electorate had forced enactment of these programs. When it was evident that most of the states would not respond to public opinion, the Federal government took over and required the states to maintain the programs under ironclad regulations and with at least half the money coming from Federal matching funds. Any deviation by a state meant an immediate shutting off of the money spigot. This was humiliating, but no other solution to human suffering and grave economic problems seemed feasible.

II

Why have the states lost so much of their sovereignty? Why do many able men contradict their own speeches by rushing pell-mell to Washington, D. C., at the first political opportunity and then rarely returning to state government after defeat at the polls?

With a few exceptions—New York being one—state government is attempting to operate with stone-age tools. Legislators who write state laws and state executives who enforce them are, for the most part, part-time officials. They can give their responsibility to the state only a lick and a promise. Other sources provide their basic incomes. Where the treasure is, there is the heart —and the vote. These men are not free to make the public interest their exclusive concern. They must cater to special interests or they don't eat. This may have been tolerable when Oregon's budget for a year was $25,000,-000. It strains matters when the budget aggregates $384,519,871.

I have sat in the Senate of my state listening to Senators who were lawyers for creameries arguing against low milk prices, and to men who were writing out life-insurance policies for timber barons pleading for a low ceiling on income taxes. A Senator who represented small-loan companies felt that 36 per cent annually was not necessarily a usurious rate of interest. Senators doubling as attorneys for utility corporations could discern

no sound reason why a power company should be denied permission to pour concrete across a mountain
stream famous for fly-fishing. Senators who were coun-
sels for real-property interests could become eloquent
in denunciation of public housing. And restrictions on
the sale of liquor made little sense to Senators who were
retained by breweries.

But are the Senators at fault or is the public the real
culprit? What about a prevailing attitude toward state
government which is so indifferent that it permits State
Senators to be paid a trifling $600 a year? If a man mak-
ing laws cannot sustain his family on the salary he receives from the state, then he must serve other masters.
Some of these masters may be pleased to have him in
their retinue if only because he can voice a *yea* or *nay*
during strategic roll calls in the State Senate. I have
watched many honest legislators sweating out a conflict
between their duty to the voters and a command from
those who supplied their daily bread. The outcome of
many such conflicts helps to explain why state government is such a gamboling ground for privilege and
monopoly.

In his autobiography *Breaking New Ground* Gifford
Pinchot has described how legislatures in the Western
states were adopting resolutions against the setting up
of Federal forest reserves, even while Congress was trying in a gingerly way to save what survived of the virgin
fir and pine. It was difficult enough to put a conservation policy through Congress, but in the legislatures it
would have been impossible. As early as Pinchot's time,
special interests had greater influence in the states than
in the national government.

And if the legislature should pass a law tinged with

idealism, would it be scrupulously enforced? In quite a few counties in our state the district attorneys have been getting $4000 annually. It is up to these men to go before the grand jury when a statute has been violated. Otherwise state law is suspended in mid-air, like Mohammed's coffin, with no application to realities.

Let me repeat an illuminating conversation with one official, a lawyer whose integrity and sincerity I would rank high. He said to me:

'Of course, I always bring to book the criminals who rob banks, assault women, and steal cars. This is simple and it also gives me headlines if I decide to run for Congress. But what if a big dairy is watering milk? Suppose a leading store is violating minimum-wage laws or elevator-safety regulations? Is the transcontinental railroad operating trains through crowded towns faster than the law allows? What if I suspect that the committee backing the successful candidate for Governor has not listed even a fraction of its total campaign expenses in our county? Is a butcher shop failing to comply with sanitary standards? Has an automobile dealer hooked his customers with repainted "lemons" by turning back speedometers and making other false representations?'

The young official continued: 'These matters involve state law. But how often do you imagine I recommend enforcement, to set an example for other wrongdoers? I am a struggling lawyer. The $333 a month from the state is just a start toward my family's expenses. The bank bandit never will be my client, the meat market might. I can't afford to offend powerful people in the community when I have to build my law practice at the same time that I serve my term. What chance do you think there is for impartial enforcement of state laws

against the high and the low alike, until folks learn that
the district attorney should serve only the public and
nobody else?'

I interrupted with a question: 'What salary do you
think a district attorney should get in this county?'

'About $12,000 a year if you want a topnotch man.'

'But that's as much as the Governor gets,' I protested.
'The voters never would stand for it.'

'Then,' answered the district attorney, 'the voters will
have to stand for the fact that state laws aren't going to
be upheld very diligently against important and influential people unless they hold up a train or pull a trigger with felonious intent.'

Only in a portion of the states of the Union do district attorneys have duties similar to those imposed
upon them in Oregon, where they must enforce regula-
tory laws as well as the criminal code. In other states,
for example, the agencies and bureaus of state government often enforce their own regulations. If court action is indicated, the Attorney-General of the state un-
dertakes the prosecution. Yet even in these states, the
practice of employing part-time district attorneys tends
to leave the local administration of justice in the hands
of men who, of necessity, cannot give it their best effort
and allegiance. Private legal clients receive the fresh
talents of these men; the state gets what remains after a
busy and exhausting schedule.

State government no longer is a casual affair. Many
state budgets are near the billion-dollar mark. A few
states have been given immense wealth in oil reserves.
The national administration is trying to give to the
states of the Far West valuable timber, grazing lands,
and water-power sites. Are decisions affecting this treas-

ure-trove to be handled with a mere lick and a promise? Lawmakers receiving $50 a month and law enforcers without a living wage are scarcely compatible with the vast responsibilities which many people hope will follow a renaissance in 'states' rights.' Can the natural resources of the country be placed in the custody of people getting coolie pay? This is an inevitable question when President Eisenhower and his associates press their belief that the states, rather than the Federal government, should hold in trust our national forests, our mountain rivers, and the continental shelf oil deposits.

III

I would list five fundamental reasons for the decline of state government in the United States, a deterioration which has accelerated in recent years. These are the reasons:

1. The part-time status and negligible salaries of state legislators and most state district attorneys.

2. The failure to reapportion legislatures so they will represent a state's population as it exists today, not as it did in the frontier past.

3. Detailed and cluttered state constitutions that lace state governments in a rigid strait jacket.

4. The one-party political domination which prevails in nearly half the states.

5. The fact that state elections are held simultaneously with Presidential elections and congressional elections.

The last point may seem innocuous, and yet it tells why the bulk of the basic problems confronting state government seldom get through to the electorate.

Nearly everywhere in the country candidates for governor and the state legislature run as Republicans or Democrats. But people judge the two parties preponderantly on such questions as the Korean war or Federal price controls or an ability to cope with the menace of Russian Communism. Occasionally some burning state issues break through the Federal curtain, but they must generate great heat to do so. Who can ignore the fact that the only Democrat to be elected governor of California in modern times was successful at the height of FDR's national glory? On the other hand, Republicans achieved their most decisive recent victories in Washington state legislative elections during 1946 and 1952, when the Democratic party was not necessarily at low ebb in the state of Washington but when it was faring badly in the country as a whole.

The late Senator George W. Norris of Nebraska put it well in the late 1920's. 'Republicans and Democrats,' he argued, 'are divided according to the views of our people on the tariff, the League of Nations, ship subsidies, and similar propositions. With these questions, the legislatures of our states have nothing whatever to do. Legislators should be elected on state issues, which are entirely different from national issues. But under present conditions, we elect a member of the legislature because he bears the label of a national party. Those who vote their ticket "straight" vote for members of the legislature on the same ticket, regardless of the fact that the voter may not agree with the candidate on any of the state issues over which the state legislature will have jurisdiction.'

Politicians being what they are, nonpartisan state government probably will come to the United States only with the millennium and the development of space suits. But a more limited proposal has been put forward by the National Municipal League, which submits that better state government will result if legislatures are elected in the odd-numbered years. This, of course, would effectively separate state and national elections.

Unless such a reform takes place, outstanding men and women are sure to be sluiced out of many state legislatures in years of national adversity for their political party. Worst of all, the cause of their defeat will be prevailing sentiment on issues wholly unrelated to state government. In the campaign of 1952 Republican candidates for the legislature in our state had one plank—Eisenhower. During the 1930's the Democratic legislative platform was equally succinct: Roosevelt.

I have a mustached friend in the parliament of one of Canada's prairie provinces. He at first refused to believe my comment that state and national elections were customarily held on the same day in the United States. 'Why,' he exclaimed, 'that's bound to put the result in the state almost completely at the mercy of the national trend! We wouldn't think of scrambling up our provincial and federal elections. They don't have any relation to each other.'

When my wife and I campaigned for the Oregon legislature, we tried to talk with our constituents about school reorganization, colored margarine, the need for state meat inspection, and consolidating counties. We were asked if, as Democrats, we went along with Acheson's ideas on Formosa and Red China and what we had to say about the scandals in the Bureau of Internal Revenue.

My wife bristles more quickly than I do. 'What do

those things have to do with the Oregon state legislature?' she asked one such interrogator.

'Well, you're both running on the Democratic ticket,'
he shot back.

A corollary of the impact of national elections on state
government is the fact that this particular dilemma exists in only about half the states. Throughout the rest
of the country the situation is, if anything, considerably
more disturbing. In approximately twenty-three or
twenty-four states not even a national political upheaval
can provide a two-party system within the legislature.
One party reigns omnipotent and its fiat stretches back
through history. We are all aware of Democratic dominance in the border states and the deep South. But not
all of us have realized that there is similarly one-party
rule in such Republican strongholds as Maine, Vermont, Iowa, Oregon, the Dakotas, and Kansas.

The Senate of Oregon, for example, has a Republican
majority that matches in lopsidedness the Democratic
clutch on the Senate of Tennessee. I am one of four
Democratic Senators in a chamber of thirty members.
Tennessee's Senate consists of twenty-eight Democrats
and five Republicans. Iowa has a State Senate of forty-
six Republicans and four Democrats. The Alabama
House of Representatives is comprised of 105 Democrats
and one forlorn Republican. North Dakota's Senate has
forty-eight Republicans and a lone Democrat, while the
lower branch of the Mississippi legislature numbers 140
Democrats and not even a solitary Republican intruder.

On a national basis the one-party states tend to cancel
out each other, which explains why the rule of neither
Democrats nor Republicans in Washington, D. C., ever
has remotely approached the political tyranny which is

the normal condition of things in many states. It also explains why the states have been so backward in responding to public opinion. Does a majority party heed popular rumblings when its hegemony is almost as secure as if held by whip and fire? The Republicans with whom I serve in the Oregon legislature are as arrogant as maharajas, and I have no doubt that my fellow Democrats in Raleigh, the state capital of North Carolina, are every bit as smug and superior.

This is the most difficult of all problems facing state government because no ready answer seems to be at hand. One-party supremacy is rooted in courthouse political rings, in vast handouts of patronage and jobs, in passions and prejudices which date back to the Civil War and the old wilderness, and in the lavish donating by special interests of a monopoly of campaign funds into the coffers of one party. Why back a hopeless cause?

Not even the national cataclysms which sway the so-called 'swing' states can crack the walls of these impregnable citadels. Oregon voted four times for Roosevelt for President, but Oregon's last Democratic legislature convened in 1878, as we know. Florida supported Eisenhower in 1952, yet the Florida State House of Representatives still has ninety-five Democrats and only five Republicans.

Thus we find that state government is determined by two strangely contrasting sets of factors: in half the states the election of the legislature and governor is dictated almost entirely by national tendencies that are remote from state affairs; and in the other half of the states, there almost might as well be no election at all, for regardless of corruption or reaction or extravagance with the taxpayers' money, the same dominant party within the state just keeps rolling along.

IV

A person unfamiliar with state constitutions would not believe what he was reading if he had thrust upon him the basic charters that govern many of the forty-eight states.

To begin with, most of these constitutions are incredibly long. Although the Constitution of the United States contains but 7500 words, the constitution of the state of Oklahoma totals 34,000 words, that of Louisiana 63,000 words, and that of California a massive 72,000 words. By attaining the length of a detective novel, a constitution inevitably will include many needless and absurd inhibitions on state government.

The constitution of Oregon restricts the location of all new state institutions such as colleges and mental hospitals to just one out of the state's thirty-six counties. The constitution of Tennessee makes ineligible for public office any individual who denies 'a system of rewards and punishments.' West Virginia's constitution bars officials of railroads from serving in the legislature. The constitution of Texas forces the state to maintain five times the number of courts and judges as serve the infinitely larger population of the United Kingdom. California's constitution goes into endless detail regarding such trivialities as the duration of wrestling matches and the breeding of mollusks and crustaceans.

Several years ago it took the vigorous efforts of California's churches, newspapers, and civic organizations to defeat a constitutional amendment that would have legalized gambling in the most audacious fashion ever proposed in this country. Written right into the amendment were the names of the five individuals who would supervise and license race tracks and slot machines in California! Had the amendment passed, these men would have become the czars of gambling in our second largest state, and the constitution would have protected them from being overruled or held in check, even by the legislature.

California has had vexing experience with the writing of personal names into its state constitution. In 1948 the electorate adopted an amendment installing a red-headed woman named Myrtle Williams, who had blue eyes and freckles, as director of social welfare at a beginning salary of $12,000. To make sure no other Myrtle Williams would mistakenly be honored, the constitution gave her exact address: 420 Avondale Street, in Monterey Park.

Because Mrs. Williams' name was rooted in the basic charter of the state, neither the governor nor the assembly at Sacramento had full control over a branch of the California government which supervises the spending of nearly $300,000,000 a year. Constitutional mandates cannot be touched or modified by the highest state officials. A costly special election finally separated Myrtle Williams from her job, although the election also diminished some needed benefits for elderly people.

Since its adoption in 1789, the United States Constitution has been amended only 22 times. Yet some state constitutions have been amended hundreds of times, and each amendment is beyond the reach of the governor and legislature. They might as well be engraved on stone, like God's commandments to Moses. 'Mine not to question why,' said the governor of a Western

state, as he surveyed a constitution in which one section
was longer than the entire Constitution of the United
States.

Arizona entered the Union as late as 1912, but 45
amendments have already been plastered onto its constitution. California's bristles with patches, 314 of them.
The constitution of Texas has been amended 104 times.

Article XIX of the 63,000-word Louisiana constitution provides: 'August 30, the birthday of Honorable
Huey P. Long, now deceased, late Governor of Louisiana, shall be and forever remain a legal holiday in this
state.' Not even George Washington's birthday is thus
sanctified by constitutional fiat in Louisiana.

Pressure groups have discovered that it is no harder
in some states to pass a constitutional amendment than
a mere law. This may be why the South Carolina constitution has 220 amendments and that of Oregon 119.
The voter, confronting a ballot the size of a hearth rug,
does not notice whether he is enacting a statute that
the legislature can revise or a constitutional clause that
will clutch state government in an immovable vise. The
authorization for cocktail bars in Oregon is written into
the constitution!

A matter locked in a state constitution is subject only
to glacial change. It takes a referendum vote among a
majority of a state's citizens to change it or set it aside.
This involves a minimum of two years' time, frequently
more. Emergencies rarely allow such a leisurely pace,
which is why the Federal government often must step
into the breach. Nor does a state referendum invariably
come out as logic seems to dictate. The constitution of
Oregon still specifies that the Governor shall be paid
$1500 a year and the State Treasurer $800. Families

with an average income of $3500 are not disposed to raise the salaries of those who govern them. Despite the plain language in the Oregon constitution, the courts have permitted the pay of officials to be increased far beyond the constitutional limits—principally, perhaps, because the state's charter similarly restricted Justices of the Oregon Supreme Court to $2000 a year apiece!

But debonairly ignoring a state constitution is not always as simple as this. Colorado's constitution requires at least 85 per cent of all state revenues from sales taxes to be reserved for old-age assistance. The well-being of the elderly is a worthy goal, but there are other deserving people in the state, too. Colorado's top position nationally in per capita payments to the aged contrasts jarringly with the fact that the ore-rich mountain state ranks sixteenth in state aid to dependent children, twenty-second in average salaries for school teachers, and twenty-sixth in general relief for distressed families. Because the legislature is powerless to readjust the distribution of state funds, the *Denver Post* has described the crisis as 'constitutional autocracy.'

Old-age assistance is a comparatively new undertaking, but a propensity for clogging state constitutions with perilous restraints on government is as old as the nation—nay, probably older. A century ago Alexis de Tocqueville was amazed to learn that the constitutions of some of the states had been written before the Constitution of the United States. And in *Democracy in America* he added, 'I am of the opinion that the Federal Constitution is superior to the constitutions of the states.'

If the prophetic Frenchman lived today, he would be reaffirmed in this conclusion. Many state constitutions confine legislatures to sessions that are two years apart. In these uncertain times, it would be difficult to plan for a pretzel factory twenty-four months ahead, let alone for a state of millions of people. Other constitutions impose an arbitrary time limit of sixty days on the length of legislative sessions. The result is a tremendous mass of bills fluttering through the chambers like confetti. Florida passed 672 laws in less than two months. The legislature of the state of Washington must act on a billion-dollar budget with indecent haste. A dozen roll calls an hour on important bills occasionally have been par for the course in the Oregon Senate. Much like Cinderella, dozens of legislatures must quit at midnight of the sixtieth day or risk having their work ruled unconstitutional. The clocks are stopped and laws enacted amidst scenes of brawling and confusion that would disgrace a Yukon saloon.

Inflexible constitutions, dating from the pioneer past, have been at the root of the virtual disenfranchisement suffered in state elections by many of America's city dwellers. In essence, these people are denied anything like their fair share of representation when state laws are written. The United States Conference of Mayors has summarized the quandary by pointing out that 60 per cent of Americans live in cities and pay nearly 90 per cent of all Federal, state, and local taxes, but receive a mere 25 per cent of the membership in the state legislatures of the nation. To this denial of city seats may be attributed the fact that state government has been loath to come to grips with such questions as housing, retarded and wayward children, race relations, traffic congestion, and consumer protection. These problems are predominantly urban in character.

Such discrepancies are often the product of constitutions that imply to counties the same standing that states enjoy in the Union. This may have been advisable when, unless the county seat was within a day's convenient travel by buckboard, people were out of touch with government. But now families span a state faster and easier than they formerly crossed a county. Yet all the counties remain—254 in Texas, 114 in Missouri, 105 in Kansas, 102 in Illinois, 99 in Iowa. Furthermore, this assigning of legislative seats to counties rather than to people occurred before the crowding of huge metropolitan areas. It was done in a period when counties were more nearly balanced in population. Salt Lake County then did not have 274,895 residents and Daggett County of Utah 364.

V

If his campaign speeches are not to be forgotten, the whole problem of ineffective state governments may have to be considered sometime by Dwight D. Eisenhower. When he was running for office, Eisenhower told the country that many duties taken on by a centralized and swollen Federal bureaucracy might best be returned to the states. He mentioned specifically public lands, water-power development, and guarantees of the rights of minorities.

Yet, as these words are written, bills setting up Fair Employment Practices Commissions have just died in the legislatures of Illinois and Missouri. What becomes of President Eisenhower's assurance that civil rights are a matter for the states if the states will not act? Nor is it without significance that the Illinois and Missouri leg-

islatures are two of the many state lawmaking bodies in
which a fair apportionment of seats had been denied for
decades.

There has been a suggestion from the national capital
that overlapping fields of taxation be eliminated. The
Federal government presumably would relinquish its
two-cents-a-gallon tax on motor fuel and perhaps the
excise taxes on cigarettes and amusement tickets. The
states, in turn, would abandon their taxes on personal
and corporate incomes. But these recommendations
have been only tentative. States that rely heavily on income taxes, such as Wisconsin and Oregon, might be
swapping a horse for a rabbit. And there is some doubt
that an Administration facing a record deficit for peacetime will surrender strategic sources of revenue.

Ultimately, the United States may decide to follow
the Canadian system of income-tax collection, under
which the government at Ottawa imposes this type of
levy and then makes rebates to the provinces. It would
have the advantage of tending to equalize the tax burden among residents of the different states. The spectacle would be gone of wealthy industrialists maintain-
ing their plants in Oregon while living across the
Columbia River in Washington, which has a sales tax
on consumers but no state levy on personal incomes.
These fortunate men buy their groceries in Oregon but
file their income-tax returns in Washington.

It is not the collection of revenue which lies at the
root of the states' difficulties, however. Money must be
collected somewhere and it is always agonizing to the
victim. This has encouraged politicians to emphasize
the fiscal phase of state problems. But to give prolonged
attention to this question would be to swat flies rather

than drain the swamp. The treatment must be more fundamental.

A model state constitution has been prepared for the National Municipal League by a committee of distinguished political scientists headed by W. Brooke Graves, chief, Government Division, of the Legislative Reference Service of the Library of Congress. Any state that adopts this constitution at least will have laid the foundation and erected the scaffolding for an effective new edifice of government.

The proposed constitution is terse and to the point. It includes a bill of rights and simple requirements for the general framework of government. The legislature would be geared to population and not to wide open spaces. It would have only one chamber, an innovation that has worked out with considerable success in Nebraska. American city councils, once saddled with two houses, now perform capably as single units. The one-house Canadian provincial parliaments have served that prospering country satisfactorily.

The model constitution also would put a strict upper limit on the number of seats in the legislature, depending to some degree on the size of the state. Thomas Jefferson counseled his friends: 'Render the legislature a desirable station by lessening the number of Representatives. Reduce your legislature to a convenient number for full but orderly discussion.'

This advice has been honored mainly in the breach. Some American legislatures are larger than Canada's national House of Commons. The New Hampshire legislature has 423 members, the Connecticut legislature 313 members, that of Massachusetts 280, and that of Pennsylvania 258.

The average legislature in the United States today totals 151 seats. The political scientists assembled by the National Municipal League recommend a quota closer to the forty-three-desk unicameral chamber in Nebraska. 'A large body of men is not deliberative,' said Senator George Norris. In the closing days of many sessions, government by mob replaces ordinary debate. Members mill around nervously.

In addition, it is impossible for the voter to follow the behavior of a horde of legislators. Victory on a ballot of bed-sheet dimensions is reduced to name familiarity. If a legislative candidate has a widely known name, he wins. In some Western states as many as 190 names have confronted the citizen on election day.

Under the model state constitution, the Governor would appoint such officials as the Secretary of State and the State Treasurer. In forty-two states at present, these men are elected. Imagine the hodgepodge in the national government if the Secretary of State and the Secretary of the Treasury were elected! Harry Truman could have found himself trying to work in harness with Joe McCarthy in charge of the State Department and Harry Byrd managing the Treasury. How would President Eisenhower team up with Wayne L. Morse as the elected Secretary of the Interior?

Yet just such internecine political warfare, on a somewhat smaller dramatic scale, frequently turns state government into chaos. The Governor must try to synchronize with heads of major departments who are after his job and trying to sabotage his politics. He cannot replace them because they owe their commissions to the electorate. Several times my state has had a Governor and State Treasurer who refused even to nod to each other.

The business of Oregon had to be conducted through intermediaries.

A new constitution could correct these situations and give a state a cabinet form of government. But how does a state get a new constitution?

The most common method is by constitutional convention. This could be promoted by the legislature or, in the twenty-six states with the initiative and referendum, the question can be placed on the ballot by petitions. But public opinion must be mobilized before the people will demand that the state acquire a modern charter, in keeping with the crucial problems of the atomic age. Trade unions, enlightened business groups, farm organizations, the League of Women Voters, and consumer co-ops can perform this job. The presence of a newspaper like the *St. Louis Post-Dispatch* or *The New York Times* or *Louisville Courier-Journal* will reinforce the effort immeasurably.

And of course a Governor with fire in his eyes and courage in his heart cannot hurt the cause. Adlai Stevenson made a first order of his administration in Illinois passage of a so-called 'gateway' amendment, opening the portals to change in a granite-anchored state constitution. For more than 40 years not an *i* had been dotted or a *t* crossed in this constitution, because any revision had to be approved by a majority of all the votes cast in an election. This was virtually impossible; too many voters never reached the measures at the bottom of the ballot. Now the Illinois constitution can be changed by a two-thirds majority of the people voting on that particular issue. Although Stevenson has gone from Springfield, the way at last is clear to giving the fourth most populous state a constitution somewhat newer than the ankle-length bathing suit.

Most of the circumstances which have put state government on the toboggan slide can be rectified through a wholesale overhauling of state constitutions. Leaders in the Council of State Governments have emphasized that this is a rare opportunity, for a man sits in the White House today who believes sincerely in widening the scope of state authority and prestige. But the electorate is sure to repudiate his philosophy in this respect if the states, given their great chance, are not equal to it. The Federal bureaucracy never has been popular per se, but the American people are hardly likely to accept in its stead either special privilege or a vacuum at the state level.

Constitution revision can provide the states with twentieth-century tools. It will not, of course, persuade men and women in the one-party states to let the hated opposition have a try. That is a matter for education and for future generations.

– 2 –

GIVE THE YOUNG FOLKS

A CHANCE

I

My wife and I are in our early forties. Although we still can climb snow-capped mountains and brave the Pacific's chilly surf, we realize that we are getting on in years. After all, each of us has been voting for two full decades. Our college days date back to the great depression, and that is now history. Yet we are younger than at least two-thirds of the other Senators and Representatives who serve with us in the legislature of a typical state of the Union.

In our opinion, youth ought to have a far greater role than this in the drafting of laws that affect such questions as child welfare, public schools, courts, mental hospitals, and the degree of financial responsibility that grown sons and daughters owe to needy parents. These often are youth's problems, but youth has only a faint voice in their solution.

State government seems upside-down to us when young legislators are merely a small and isolated minority. My wife and I wish that we qualified, even at our present ages, not as comparatively junior members of Oregon's legislature but as its venerated elders. Yet the political deck frequently is stacked against the presence of young men and women in the state capitols of our forty-eight states.

Paltry legislative salaries act as one of the principal barriers to participation in politics by the youthful citizen just starting out in life, with his fortune yet to earn. My wife, Maurine, and I, for example, are paid $600 apiece as state legislators. This annual salary barely takes care of our room rent and food during a session. Mrs. Neuberger, tired and tense in the evening after long hours spent presiding over the House Education Committee, must cook dinner because legislative pay in America is not geared to the cost of restaurant meals. And we make it a policy to decline most of the invitations which flood in on all legislators from the lobbyists for special interests.

Yet many states pay even smaller salaries than does Oregon. A man or woman who passes laws to govern Connecticut's 2,010,000 people is believed to be worth only $300 a year. Rhode Island pays $5 a day for the task of enacting statutes. This also is the daily legislative wage in the vast agricultural states of Kansas and North Dakota. In oil-rich Texas the Senators and Representatives receive $10 a day, in Wyoming $12, in Oklahoma $15. New Hampshire rewards its lawmakers with a trifling $100 a year.

This pay for legislators, less than the going rate for janitors in most capitol buildings, is at the root of much of the dry-rot eroding state government, as I shall try to demonstrate later on.

The meager pay also helps to bar from public service young men with skimpy bank accounts. I remember sitting in a pyramidal tent on a bleak December day when it was 40° below zero at Whitehorse, along the Alcan Highway. 'Just wait till a few years after this war winds up,' said the leathery staff sergeant from the Montana uplands. 'You'll see the young fellows, the fellows who've been in the war, taking charge in the United States. They'll get into politics and crowd out the old men who've been running things to suit themselves.'

I've often wondered what became of that sergeant. He was quite a fellow. He could keep a bulldozer going when a lynx didn't dare leave its lair. Unfortunately, the sergeant's prophecy was wrong. I even have speculated on whether the miserly pay of $10 a day kept him from entering the legislature of his own state. He had a tall, redheaded girl in Missoula he kept talking about. He showed her picture to everyone. I imagine they have a family now. What honest lawmaker can feed and clothe a family on $10 a day?

My wife and I definitely refuse to string along with the ancient Greek notion of 'old men for council, young men for war.' Young men—and young women, too—should sit in their country's councils, and a state legislature is the place to begin.

This is the predominant reason that we support the program of the National Muncipal League, an organization crusading for good government, which insists that 'in no case should legislative compensation ever be less than $4000 a year.' Present pay scales are particularly hard on the young citizen in politics, who rarely has enough of a financial backlog to tide him through three or four months of legislating at less than a golf-caddy rate of compensation.

But some progress has been made. A few years ago Michigan's lawmakers received $3 a day for each day the legislature was in session. Now the pay in Michigan is up to $2400 annually. The state of Washington in 1949 paid $300 for a legislative session of sixty days, but by 1953 the salary had been increased to $1200.

The National Municipal League, however, feels even this pay is inadequate. John E. Bebout, one of its staff consultants, has claimed that 'it is contrary to all this country stands for to bar a young lawyer or mechanic or farmer from public service because he has a slender wallet.' Yet, contrast the $1200 a year paid to legislators in the wealthy manufacturing state of Indiana with the $3000 paid to lawmakers on the hungry island of Puerto Rico!

II

Some of our colleagues in the tree-dotted Oregon capital city of Salem are almost twice as old as we are. The average age of members of our legislature is forty-nine, a situation identical with that in many other states. This nearly equals the average age in the national Congress—fifty-three. But our forty-eight legislatures, with a grand total of 7,234 Senators and Representatives, ought to be where young citizens are preparing for future Congressional experience in Washington, D. C.

Can anything be done about youth's skimpy quota of seats? We firmly believe young men and women of courage and integrity will become legislative candidates if the salaries are more in keeping with modern living costs, if the voters give closer attention to who represents them in the state capitol, and if there is tighter control of big campaign slush funds.

Youth's natural idealism sometimes tends to shrink from the grim realities of present-day politics. A thirty-one-year-old ex-bomber pilot from World War II, who was practicing law in a small town in California, said to me, 'I'd run for the legislature in a minute if I thought I could vote just as my conscience dictated, without having to worry about campaign contributors or the bosses of my party.'

This was how I replied to him: 'Maybe a whole lot of young men like you will have to run first, in order to bring about the conditions which you seek. When you don't even put your name on the ballot, you leave the business of state government to the political hacks. One of the important things you could work for might be a law requiring full exposure of all political campaign donations from the underworld and other shady sources.'

In 1948 my wife and I begged and pleaded with a former college chum in his late thirties to run for the State Senate from the timbered Oregon seacoast.

'This county hasn't elected a Democratic Senator for half a century,' said Bob Holmes, who directs amateur theatricals, wins golf tournaments, and manages a radio station.

'They'll elect you," I rashly predicted. 'They want some new blood in the legislature.'

As a freshman Senator, Bob was able to defeat a series of bills which imperiled the spectacular Chinook salmon runs that support hundreds of fishermen and cannery workers in his county. Now he can stay in the legislature as long as he desires—or, I tell him, until some younger man with bright new ideas challenges his supremacy.

I have been an Oregon State Senator for five years, winning a seat for the first time after my return from Army duty at lonely Whitehorse on the headwaters of the Yukon River. My wife entered the other branch of the legislature as a Representative in 1950. We were both re-elected last November. The Council of State Governments revealed that never before had a husband and wife been elected simultaneously to both houses of an American legislature.

Our legislative experience has convinced both of us that the average age of lawmakers at the state level ought to be no higher than forty. Better still, it might be thirty-seven or thirty-eight, for even this average would leave room for quite a few older members.

Such a prevailing age could be far too young, some may claim. It requires wisdom and maturity to pass laws. Yet if any place should be hospitable to young Americans just starting their political careers, it is a state legislature. This tradition is rooted securely in the history of the United States. It once was as normal for future statesmen to begin in their home legislatures as it is now for the next generation of major-league baseball players to commence on the neighborhood sand lot.

Thomas Jefferson was only thirty-three when he sat in Virginia's House of Burgesses. In fact, it was during this legislative term that he wrote the immortal Declaration of Independence. At twenty-five, Abraham Lincoln was a Representative in the legislature of Illinois and the floor-manager of his party. Theodore Roosevelt had just turned twenty-four when, as a member of the New York Assembly, he exposed corruption among a group of notorious financiers. Teddy's distant cousin, Franklin Delano Roosevelt, reached the Senate of the same legislature by the time he was twenty-eight.

But the more recent leaders of America have not traveled this well-worn trail. Few Presidential nominees of late years ever served in a state legislature—not Dwight D. Eisenhower, not Harry Truman, not even men who were nominated directly from state governorships, like Thomas E. Dewey and Adlai Stevenson.

In this era we frequently leave service in our legislatures to hardened political professionals, to men turned gray and cynical in the stubborn game of vote-getting. This helps to explain the lack of confidence which the average citizen often betrays toward state government.

Yet Americans all through the years have hungered for young candidates. Lincoln went triumphantly to Springfield after his opponent had ridiculed him as too immature and untried for a desk in the State House of Representatives.

'The gentleman has seen fit to allude to my being a young man,' said the tall, lean prairie lawyer who had just passed his twenty-fifth birthday. 'But he forgets that I am older in years than I am in the tricks and trades of politicians.'

The voters of Sangamon County howled gleefully. They wanted a young lawmaker and Lincoln had shrewdly emphasized the fact that his aged adversary was a professional politician.

III

But why don't more young citizens sit in our legislatures today?

Many give up before they start. They develop a defeatist complex about the old hands at politics whom they generally must oppose. They decide that their chances are slim against such competition.

I am sure these are phantom fears. Given a clear choice, the voters ordinarily will send a young man or woman to the paneled chambers in the state capitol building. In 1948, just before my wife baked my favorite caramel cake with thirty-six candles, I ran 24,000 votes ahead of a veteran politician who was almost twice my age.

At the time my wife Maurine filed her candidacy for the House of Representatives, we were besieged with warnings that this would beat both of us. The voters, we were told, never would stand for a husband and wife serving together in the legislature. The resentment might eliminate us from politics permanently. In a moment of panic we considered withdrawing Maurine's name, but finally decided to stick by our intention of winning or losing together.

A man with a reputation for being one of Oregon's cagiest political observers said to us, 'Folks will be indignant over the presence of two Neubergers on the same ballot, especially because neither one of you is as seasoned or experienced as most of the other members of the legislature.'

But the attitude of the voters seemed more accurately reflected in the letter that I received from a young working mother, who lives in a small crossroads community just outside Portland.

'I intend to vote for both you and your wife,' she wrote, 'because I am glad to see a woman at last get equal recognition along with her husband. She isn't going to be your secretary or committee clerk, or anything like that. She is going to try to be a legislator in her own right, just like you. That appeals to all of the people I know here in our little town. We also hope that she shows her independence by voting opposite to you on some of the bills before the legislature.'

Maurine and I had a vivid demonstration of the fact that the electorate, even in a conservative state such as Oregon, has no objection to candidates who are young in spirit. My wife had taught physical education in the public schools and she still participates in modern-dance programs. In addition, she is an active swimmer. This meant that pictures of her in bathing suits and a tight-fitting black leotard had been published.

Several of her opponents circulated these clippings and put to voters a question: 'Do you want a woman to represent you in the legislature who allows her picture to appear barelegged in the newspapers in a bathing suit?'

This criticism boomeranged. My wife sweetly reminded her critics that one of Oregon's principal enterprises was the manufacturing of knitted bathing suits, with wool from the sheep which graze on the high green mountain meadows. Surely, said Maurine, her political opponents did not think every woman who patronized this great home industry was automatically ineligible for a seat in the legislature!

Maurine polled more votes last November than ever before had been received by a female candidate running for legislative office anywhere in our state. She was especially successful in districts where her dancing and athletic activities had been assailed. Indeed, a prominent Protestant clergyman said to her:

'I'm sure that a good many voters right in my own congregation aren't ashamed of the fact that they have a lady legislator at the capital who has a good figure. They also know that "evil is as evil thinks." We're glad our legislator is graceful enough and still young enough to do leaps and pirouettes, in addition to passing laws!'

Every tangible bit of evidence strengthens our belief that youth in ideas, as well as in years, appeals to the American people.

When Maurine was sponsoring a bill to legalize colored margarine, she strode before the Agricultural Committee in a zebra-striped apron which covered her from throat to knees. In her arms she carried a big kitchen mixing bowl. While the other legislators gasped in astonishment, she showed the members of the committee the messy chore that Oregon laws imposed on the average housewife. It was not lost on her that the entire committee was made up of farmers. Perhaps they never had seen oleo hand-mixed before.

After Maurine's hour-long appearance with yellow pellets and greasy fingers, the foes of colored margarine said she had killed her own cause. 'Too undignified a stunt in a legislative chamber,' claimed a leading dairy lobbyist. 'People don't want their $3,000,000 marble capitol turned into a public kitchen.'

But the episode had an opposite effect on housewives. It stirred them to action. Their letters and telegrams cascaded across desks in the Senate and House. Even rural legislators, who a few weeks earlier had denounced colored margarine as if it were vodka imported from Soviet Russia, had to go back on their strident words. Oregon's prohibition against the sale of yellow margarine, which had existed for 38 years, was overwhelmingly repealed.

IV

At least twenty states are dominated by one political party,* which consistently wins most offices. This discourages many young men and women in the minority party. They decide public life is not for them, and they never make the test.

We are convinced this surrender is a mistake. Oregon has not had a Democratic legislature since 1878. Yet Maurine and I, both Democrats, were the only legislative nominees to run substantially ahead of General Eisenhower in November of 1952, in any district in our Republican state.

The normal American is not a rabid partisan. He votes for the candidate rather than the party. Zealous partisans make the noise, but they have no louder voice than anyone else on election day. Again and again, we addressed Republicans who gave us a friendly hearing and promised support if our ideas made sense.

A candidate will fare better with independent voters if he is not the victim of an attitude of 'my party, right or wrong.' My wife and I have bucked the Democratic

* I have listed as one-party states those with legislatures where the minority party has less than 20 per cent of the total membership. This would establish the following as one-party states dominated by the Democrats: Alabama, Arkansas, Florida, Georgia, Louisiana, Mississippi, North Carolina, Oklahoma, South Carolina, Tennessee, Texas, and Virginia. Under this formula, one-party states ruled by the Republicans would be Iowa, Kansas, Maine, New Hampshire, North Dakota, Oregon, South Dakota, and Vermont. In rare or unusual circumstances, a Democrat sometimes wins a major office in these Republican states and occasionally a Republican nominee for President may win the electoral votes of one of the Democratic states. But the prevailing one-party hegemony has seldom been permanently disturbed.

party organization on the issue of county consolidation. Oregon has thirty-six counties, most of them created before the railroads came. We think the state could get by with no more than eight counties. Our party leaders don't like the plan because they hope to take over some of the plush county offices for the Democrats. We are sure that our political independence on this question has helped us with the rank and file of voters.

But many politicians, on the job for successive decades, have a granite resistance to change. When I sponsored a bill in the State Senate to increase legislative pay in Oregon to a modest $1200 a year, one wealthy gray-haired Senator said, 'I don't think a man should come to this chamber until he can afford it.'

But what about the young citizen interested in government, who has not had enough time to build up a bank account? In the House of Representatives my wife sits next to a thirty-four-year-old lawyer named Pat Dooley. He tells her that he often is unable to decide between attending an important legislative hearing at night or working far into the morning hours on a legal brief or contract.

'I can't let my law practice go to rack and ruin,' explains Pat, who has a wife and two children. "I might not have any livelihood at all to go back to after the session is over. While I sit at the legislature, my office rent continues and so does the mortgage on our house. It adds a real mental hazard, I tell you, to the job of making up my mind on how I should vote on each bill that comes before us.'

In our capitol building with its fluted dome, stenographers and electricians and custodians are paid more than Senators and Representatives. This tends to belittle and shame the process of enacting laws at the state level. It makes the ordinary citizen think that the legislature is of scant consequence. Who could possibly be doing anything important for $600 a year? A barmaid or busy baby-sitter might earn more than that!

Fortunately, many civic organizations throughout the nation are crusading vigorously for adequate legislative salaries. They also are turning their attention to such companion problems as the $4500 annual pay of the Governor of Maryland. Even the emoluments and allowances provided for expenses do not detract from the absurdity of giving the chief executive of a state of 2,400,000 people a pay check totaling less than $400 a month.

High-school teachers complain that scarcely any of their students, even in the senior grades, can name a state legislator from their own county. We are told by a college political science professor that many of his students can identify bygone members of Britain's Parliament but not present members of Oregon's legislature! I know State Senators who have been in diligent and faithful attendance at a session of the legislature and then had people in their home community ask seriously, 'Where you been keeping yourself? Haven't seen you lately.'

What the legislature does may seem remote and of no significance to you and your family. We thought this, too—until we saw at first hand the questions decided by legislative action in a typical state.

If you are concerned about the schools where your children are enrolled, don't forget that the legislature fixes teachers' pay and tenure and the number of days of their sick-leave. It may shape the boundaries of school districts and even pass on curriculum and textbooks. It decides whether school buildings must be fireproof and whether school playgrounds ought to be green lawn or hard asphalt.

Worried over the roads and streets that you travel with your car? The legislature sets gasoline taxes and distributes this huge revenue among the cities and counties of the state. It determines the number of State Police available for highway patrol. It decides whether the jobs of the troopers shall be at the mercy of politics or protected by civil service. The legislature dictates what extra amount big trucks and trailers will pay, if anything, for the pummeling they give pavement and bridges.

Do you ever wonder if the produce in the supermarket is sanitary? It's up to the legislature to require physical examinations for food handlers, to settle such matters as weights and labeling, and to decide whether there will be inspection of the barns where dairy cows are milked.

No day of a legislative session reaches sundown without our marveling at the countless issues we decide that touch intimately the lives of every family in the state.

Oregon had a horse-meat scandal. People who thought they were serving ground round steak to their youngsters actually had been buying chopped-up pieces of mares and stallions. All at once we discovered that there was no Oregon law requiring inspection of meat wholly produced inside the state. Foul and inferior cuts unable to qualify for interstate shipment were being sold within our own borders. The consumer had no protection. We quickly introduced a bill in the legislature to close this glaring breach. That the bill failed of passage affirmed our conviction that citizens pay too little attention to their state capital. Its passage could have been assured by the slightest pressure from the men and women whose health would be endangered by contaminated beef or pork.

Because so many of these major problems confront young men and women, we frequently are distressed at the relatively few youthful members in the legislature.

My wife had just written a bill to allow working mothers to deduct for tax purposes, the money they must spend for child care during the hours in which they are employed. Oregon has one of the stiffest state income taxes in the country. To Maurine's desk came a steady torrent of letters indicating how much the success of her bill could mean to innumerable young families, who now must pay a substantial portion of their earnings to housekeepers or baby-sitters.

'Isn't it a tragic and ironic thing,' my wife asked after such a day, 'that many of the people who approach me with real troubles for the legislature to solve, never even voted at all in the legislative brackets on the ballot at the last election?'

v

In spite of the desire of the average citizen to be represented by young legislators, many political situations are deliberately rigged against the newcomer to public life.

One such condition is the vexing need for a big campaign fund. Special interests sometimes hesitate to finance a young candidate if they fear he will be hard to handle when a favor is wanted at the expense of the general public. Morty Freedman, political reporter of the *St. Petersburg Times,* has estimated the cost of winning a legislative seat in Pinellas County, Florida, at 'somewhere between $5000 and $10,000.' What do groups putting up this money expect of a legislator, whose own pay from the state of Florida will be a meager $10 a day?

In Oregon candidates have had war chests of $3000, a sum five times the annual legislative salary. Some of these funds are contributed by forces that seek special legislation regarding taxes, slot machines, public forest lands, or state contracts. A young nominee without such a campaign exchequer frequently finds that his opponent is smothering him with an avalanche of billboards, direct-mail brochures, and paid precinct workers.

Ever since I came to the State Senate I have sponsored bills to limit the funds that can be spent in political campaigns and to require public reporting before election day of the sources of all these funds. My proposals would give the Director of Elections authority to undertake detailed audits, to make sure that political contributions from the underworld were not concealed or camouflaged.

Such reforms, in my opinion, will help to keep more nearly equal the competition between professional politicians and forthright young newcomers. As we shall see, however, no reform is more difficult to achieve. Politicians hesitate to change the rules under which they themselves have prospered!

Politics is a rough pastime, but the goal of the honest citizen in politics is a noble one. That goal is good government. I know of no better place to work actively toward such a goal than in an American state legislature. I know of no place where ability and courage are so desperately needed. Our legislatures face stern questions, but they lack the necessary talent and vigor.

I remember a public hearing at which Maurine presided as chairman of the Education Committee of the House of Representatives. The question at issue was a state-supported university for Portland, the only large city in the West without such an institution.

One by one, parents in straitened financial circumstances got up before the committee and told how their children never could go to college unless the bill was passed. These fathers and mothers could not afford to send the teen-agers in their families to a far-off campus. In order to receive an education, their sons and daughters had to be able to live at home. They also needed the part-time jobs which a big city offered.

The hall was full of hundreds of high-school seniors. They listened intently. Their opportunity to be a surgeon or a chemist or a teacher was being decided, right in that hearing chamber. One could feel the tension and anxiety. The speakers addressed the legislative committee with a new intensity and fervor. Why should Portland, alone, be without a state college? A young lawyer, a veteran of the Korean fighting, put this question in urgent tones which stirred even the drowsiest committee member.

This was the right of petition, the right of citizens to voice an appeal to their government. Another young man, Jefferson, had written movingly about this basic right when America as a nation was very young, indeed.

That night, as we walked to our rented cottage in the state capital city of Salem, my wife said to me: 'For the first time I think I really appreciate what a wonderful thing it is to participate in politics and government in the United States. Why, if we pass this bill for a college, we'll be giving countless boys and girls a better chance in life. Think of what that means! That's real and tangible. All of a sudden, my election to the legislature seems more important to me than it ever has before.'

I looked behind us for a moment. In the distance Oregon's soaring capitol dome pointed upward to the stars.

– 3 –

MRS. NEUBERGER RINGS THE

POLITICAL GONG

I

PEOPLE will wonder how the wife of a man in politics gets into the act herself. What impelled State Senator Neuberger's spouse to become Representative Neuberger?

To tell the truth, I am a little stunned by it all, too—especially the success of the experiment.

'Experiment' it most certainly was, for the Council of State Governments could find no previous record of a husband and wife serving simultaneously in the two branches of a state legislature.

In the 1952 election I was particularly apprehensive about the project. How would two Neubergers fare in the same district? Would the voters think it was an overdose? My fears were prodded by the fact that an Eisenhower landslide seemed possible, and Democrats in Oregon ran none too well even under favorable circumstances.

The big Eisenhower avalanche materialized, but

45

Douglas McKean in the *Journal* of Portland referred to a 'little Neuberger landslide' as well. In Multnomah County, which includes Portland and a fringe of farms and bustling small towns, General Ike polled 132,602 votes. Among the thirty-six legislative candidates of both parties on the ballot, only two received more votes than Eisenhower. Maurine's total was 133,467, mine was 145,796. All the rest trailed the General by a substantial margin.

The experiment had worked. A husband and wife could try it together and the voters would approve, generously. When my friend Palmer Hoyt of the *Denver Post* introduced me at a banquet of journalists he announced he had just learned that Mr. and Mrs. Neuberger constituted, between them, 15 per cent of the entire Democratic Party membership in the Oregon Legislature.

'We've all heard of the political party that was so bad off it could caucus in a phone booth,' said Mr. Hoyt, 'but, by the lord Harry, this is the first time I've ever heard of a political party that could caucus in bed!'

The *Post's* distinguished publisher was referring to the fact that only two Democratic State Senators and ten Democratic State Representatives ran the Eisenhower gantlet in Oregon, and Maurine and I were among them. We were worse off than the Republicans in some of the states of the deep South.

How did it really happen? It really happened because of my wife. When the experiment began, it was all up to her. If she made good, we both made good. If she flopped, we flopped together. We ran ahead of General Ike because Maurine wowed the state in her first term as a Representative, which began in 1950. She also taught the people of Oregon—and her husband—a lot about what a woman could accomplish in government.

One of my Senate colleagues remarked: 'Your wife stole the show right out from under your nose at this session.' And so indeed she had. Since 1915, the sale of colored margarine had been forbidden in Oregon. Now my wife had led a crusade which ended the ban, and she had been rewarded with enthusiastic cheers from the press and from thousands of families.

A few months earlier, this would have given me agonizing twinges of jealousy. Although my wife could excel in the kitchen, I did not want her to encroach on my own particular domain, which happened to be the state legislature. But at last I have learned that my wife is a person in her own right, that she is as entitled to recognition as I am. When she abandoned her name and took mine, she did not similarly put behind her all independent claims to fame and achievement. And if my wife's bid for accomplishment took place in an area where I had been predominant—well, that was something I would have to grin and bear.

It was on a trip to the Clearwater National Forest solitudes of neighboring Idaho that I was suddenly confronted by the decision of accepting my wife as a partner in practice as well as in theory. She looked up one brisk morning from the sourdough biscuits she was baking and casually announced:

'I'd like to run for the legislature myself this year. I have some pretty good ideas and I might as well be speaking for them on the floor as knitting up in the gallery.'

No complacent male ever was taken more completely by surprise. My wife previously had seemed quite content with reflected glory; occasionally she took a bow in my behalf. But always it was evident who was at the helm. I was master, she was mate. Now she proposed to put her hand beside mine on the wheel spokes of government. It was a jolt.

I wandered up a foaming creek, sat on a ledge, and did some hard thinking. Could my wife be trusted to make delicate political judgments? What if she did something to embarrass me? Could I allow a promising career to be nipped at the source merely because my wife was ambitious to serve in the Legislature, too? I trudged back toward camp, determined to put an end to such nonsense. But as I walked along, another thought struck me. Did not my wife have the right to precisely the same attitude? After all, Article XIX of the Constitution had given women the vote and made them the political equals of men. Did I have the privilege, even within our household, to set aside this great mandate?

That night, in the glow of a kerosene lamp in our tent, I helped my wife fill out her application for a place on the Oregon ballot. We mailed it next dawn down the trail at the Ranger Station. No deed has ever returned such rich and heart-warming dividends.

I have discovered that my wife is every bit as skillful and competent at politics as I am. And yet, in no field does the American male consider himself so traditionally superior. I had a generous portion of this male ego when my wife's bill legalizing yellow margarine came up for debate.

'Here is your speech for tomorrow,' I said, handing her a bulky sheaf. 'You say these things and you won't go wrong.'

My wife took the document politely and sat down to

read it. As I fell asleep that night, I heard her busily pecking away on a portable typewriter.

Next day I sat back comfortably, waiting to hear my words spoken by my wife during the debate. She started somewhat differently, but I put this down to the fact that she had altered the introduction. Then she began to get into the main body of the speech. Still my material did not come. And finally I realized that the words being spoken were entirely her own. And I noticed that the other legislators were listening attentively.

When it was over the President of the Senate, who took the other side of the margarine issue, said to me: 'That's one of the finest, most logical talks I ever heard in the legislature!'

Starting with that episode, my wife and I became legislative partners. We were a team, and she called the signals as often as I did. We talked over important bills and frequently it was her judgment that prevailed.

To begin with, her outlook was never clouded by further political ambitions. On her desk she kept a little motto, attributed to the late U. S. Senator Claude Swanson of Virginia: 'When in doubt, do right.' She quoted it to me when we were wondering whether to oppose a bill that sharply reduced state funds for dependent children.

I was afraid that old-age pensioners might be angry because their appropriations benefited from this reduction. After all, elderly folks voted, but children didn't.

My wife looked at me sharply. 'Let's just do right,' she said.

I never regretted the decision, and the pensioners turned out to be nobler about the matter than I had thought.

I had worried that the presence of my wife on the ballot might imperil my own political plans. Yet to my desk flowed a stream of letters from women, expressing appreciation that at least one husband had seen fit to share his career with his wife. I am looking at one of these letters now:

'I think every housewife has a right to participate in government if she has the ability to do so. We are not mere cooks and bottle washers. I am glad you are setting so fine an example for other husbands in our state.'

II

Demagoguery ill suits a woman. A male politician may get by with stem-winding speeches that sound like a steam calliope. Such a performance from a woman would be regarded as practically a vaudeville act. Her contribution must be the short, pithy observation that gets right down to brass tacks. Equivocation may promote the ambitions of the male officeholder, but the woman is best off when she speaks her mind.

Maurine never equivocates. Occasionally her blunt answers make me wince. I am accustomed to more 'strategy.' Yet I think this is why she has been successful. Nor does she make the mistake of sounding off whenever the fancy strikes her.

In politics, long considered a realm exclusively for males, the woman intruder is most effective when she is seen but rarely heard. This does not mean she should be a cipher—far from it. But she must make every verbal missile count. If she even remotely confirms the legend of the clacking female, her usefulness is at an end.

Most male politicians believe, in their smug superiority, that women know nothing of politics. This has its advantages, for the woman. She can make a statement which would be looked upon as heresy coming from an elective official in trousers, yet in her is attributed to naïveté or lack of 'experience.'

For example, the dairy interests long have been practically sacrosanct in our state. Both our United States Senators, including the intrepid and liberal Wayne Morse, opposed removal of the punitive Federal tax on butter's cheaper rival, oleomargarine. After Maurine had risen to her feet in the State Assembly and cited Department of Agriculture figures to prove that Oregon dairy distributors were punishing the housewife with the highest retail prices charged anywhere along the Pacific Coast for milk, one of her awed male colleagues confided to her: 'What you said is true, but only a woman could make such a statement in this Capitol building—and get away with it.'

Once a woman gets into office, she usually surprises even skeptics. Connecticut Republicans broke precedent and chose a woman to be Secretary of State. This woman, Alice Leopold, did such a good job that a large segment of the party rebelled when a member of the male sex was nominated to succeed her. Maurine had a similar experience. People all over the state protested at the time it was rumored that a certain candidate for Speaker of the House planned to replace Mrs. Neuberger as chairman of the Committee on Education. 'We'll boycott the Legislature!' threatened one loyal PTA leader in the southern part of the state.

In politics, the woman's mission is to champion the particular aspirations of her sex, but to expect no quarter in doing so. She is in for a grim awakening if she enters public life thinking her male associates will defer to her opinions merely because she is a woman. Superficial amenities she will receive by the score, but these often will cloak the grimmest kind of opposition to her cherished legislative proposals.

Maurine's male associates bow and scrape when merely the social graces are at stake. She is 'our fair and lovely colleague' or 'the gentlewoman from Multnomah County.' She sits by common consent at the head table at banquets. No one lets her carry her own briefcase through the marble corridors. Representatives rise when she enters the members' lounge. On the surface, her every wish is a command.

She thought so, too—at first. Then, one emotion-fraught afternoon, she appealed from a ruling of the chair. Someone had to second her appeal to carry the issue to a vote.

Robert's Rules of Order later proved to be on her side, but the fifty-nine males in the chamber, Republicans and Democrats alike, sat on their hands and stilled their voices. The danger flags were flying. No longer was Maurine a mere female in a fluffy blouse and sheer hose. This was womankind challenging man's inherent right to rule. And chivalry died right then and there.

The woman who enters politics must be feminine, yet firm. Without sacrificing any of the qualities that make a woman attractive in a man's eyes, she must stand by her convictions and uphold the interests of her sex. And when questions involving economic dominance and political power are at issue, not only will she receive no preference because of her sex, but she probably will be considered fair game for that reason.

This has been demonstrated in greater political arenas than the Oregon State Legislature. Not even Senatorial

Maurine and Richard Neuberger are the first husband-and-wife team in American history ever elected simultaneously to both chambers of a state legislature.

The senator and the representative
work up a bill in the law library.

seniority kept Margaret Chase Smith of Maine from losing an important committee assignment as a result of her rebuke to Senator McCarthy. And one of the most bitter campaigns of vilification in the annals of the Pacific Coast helped bring about the defeat of Helen Gahagan Douglas for the Senate in California by Richard Nixon, now the Vice President.

Gossip, much of it malicious, has been the servant of politics from time immemorial. If to a man it can be an annoyance and matter of concern, to a woman it can be far worse.

Politics are as close as we come to war in our normal peacetime lives. The 'killer instinct' to destroy an adversary is rarely suspended because the adversary happens to wear skirts and bear children. In a nice, smiling sort of way, the American woman in politics must not let herself be pushed around.

After Maurine had written to the daily paper in a nearby city questioning the vote of the local legislator on an issue of interest to women, he came to her with the clipping in his hand. 'I'm getting lots of mail from housewives because of your letter,' he said angrily. 'I don't think that was a very ladylike thing for you to do.'

'Perhaps it wasn't,' Maurine replied sweetly. 'But if you were a gentleman, would you have voted against a lady's bill?'

That stopped him. In her own charming way, Maurine has not let herself be pushed around by her male colleagues.

When she introduced a bill providing for tax deductions of money spent for baby-sitters, the measure promptly was buried in the tax committee. But Maurine was stubbornly convinced of the rightness of her cause.

After all, corporations were deducting liquor, fan danc-
ers, World Series tickets, and standby airplanes. Why
shouldn't a working mother be allowed to subtract the
money she spent on child care?

'What's more important in the scheme of things in
our state tax structure?' asked Maurine at the Federated
Women's Club. 'Is it entertaining a prospective client
or raising the next generation?'

To the banner of the 'baby-sitting bill,' Maurine rallied waitresses, schoolteachers, laundry workers, bar-
maids, and farm mothers who had to milk cows or run
tractors. Letters came in great numbers across her desk.
She and her secretary practically had to bale them; they
were too numerous to file. Still, Maurine made no move.

Then, with the legislative session nearly at an end,
she went to members of the tax committee with a few
of her letters. She faced these individuals pleasantly.
'Perhaps you can advise me about replying to this mail,'
she suggested. 'I'm rather inexperienced, and I don't
quite know how to tell these women that the baby-sitting bill has been tabled in committee. They'll be aw-
fully disappointed, you know.'

Nor did Maurine neglect to remind each committee
member that a generous portion of the letters from
irate mothers originated in his own county.

Some of these legislators were inflexible reactionaries.
Their ideas were rooted in granite as unyielding as the
ramparts of Mount Hood, which gleamed dazzlingly east
of the Willamette Valley. But the committee members
got Maurine's point. Come the next election day, the
working mothers with youngsters would not forget.

When the omnibus tax measure was reported to the
House shortly before final adjournment, the baby-sitting

bill introduced by Maurine was part of it. She did not get quite all she wanted. But the bill provided for deductions of up to $60 a month for money 'paid for the care of dependent children.'

And this was how Oregon became the first state in the Union to adopt a principle with respect to its income tax that women's groups had sought everywhere in the nation for more than a decade.

III

Today I get as much satisfaction from my wife's achievements as from my own. I glory in the fact that a woman has invaded a man's world successfully, and that the woman happens to be my wife. And I observe that others beneath the capitol dome increasingly consult her on strategy and plans.

No longer is there any doubt that my wife is a more effective legislator than I am. She has passed more bills and won more converts for her causes. Her friendly, somewhat shy personality has triumphed where the more bellicose masculine approach has stumbled.

Now that my wife has finally been emancipated from her husband's fears, I am learning new things about her all the time. On a recent vacation trip in the Cascade Range, several of us were speculating how to recapture a fishing raft that had drifted far from shore on a mountain lake dotted with floating ice.

Without a word, my wife went into a tent and emerged in her black bathing suit, with the Red Cross emblem on the bosom. Then she swam with long, vigorous strokes through the frigid water to the raft.

'I didn't know your wife could swim quite like that,' said a friend.

'I didn't either,' I replied. 'In fact, I've learned a lot about my wife this past year, and it's my own fault that I didn't realize her capabilities a long time ago.'

All I can wonder is how many women in the U. S. are hiding genuine talents because jealous husbands resent any challenge to their family supremacy, whether it is in a legislative hall or beside a wilderness lake.

– 4 –

WHY DON'T 'BETTER' PEOPLE

GET INTO POLITICS?

I

My wife and I sat at the end of a long conference table in the new Student Union Building of the University of Washington. Sunlight streamed in through the arched Tudor-Gothic windows. In the distance shimmered a gleaming lake, dotted with motorboats. Beyond the lake rose the dark, timbered foothills of the Cascade Range.

But we were not there to look at scenery. We were facing two dozen political science teachers from the leading colleges of the Northwest. They hammered at us questions about practical politics—questions based on our service in the Oregon State Legislature.

'Where did you get the money for your campaigns?'

'Have you been able to vote your own honest views?'

'Do you recommend people for state jobs because of their ability or because of their political affiliations?'

'Are genuine ethics and morality possible in public life today?'

'Does an unknown young candidate have a real chance of election?'

'Does participation in politics result in personal unhappiness and frustrated ambitions?'

Our presence at the end of that table, where we could be questioned by the region's teachers of political science, was part of an extraordinary project sponsored by an outstanding American, who lives on the opposite side of the continent.

Arthur T. Vanderbilt, Chief Justice of the state of New Jersey and one of the most distinguished lawyers of this generation, long has been alarmed over the way the 'better' people in most communities shun politics as if it were contaminated.

By 'better' Justice Vanderbilt does not imply, of course, superiority in wealth, social position, or fame. His use of the phrase 'better minds for better politics' has specific reference to intelligence, education, integrity, and general traits of character. By this definition the son of a locomotive engineer or dirt farmer might be more qualified for public life than the legatee of a millionaire. All too often, in Justice Vanderbilt's opinion, the people of decency, knowledge, and trustworthiness leave the important business of government to their inferiors in these basic essentials.

As a past president of the American Bar Association, as an active Methodist, and as an eminent dean of the Law School of New York University, Justice Vanderbilt has been disturbed by 'the strange antipathy to politics which permeates the social environment of our young people.' Himself the father of five children, he spares none of his own realms in making the indictment:

'This antipathy to politics is reflected in the home,

the church and the school. In a recent national poll it was reported that 69 per cent of our people did not want their children to enter politics, and almost 50 per cent thought no man could be in politics and remain honest. . . Only rarely do we find an awareness in academic circles, for example, that we live in an age of politics, of power politics, that affects quite literally almost every phase of life.'

Justice Vanderbilt's answer has been the founding of the Citizenship Clearing House, with the aid of funds from the Maurice and Laura Falk Foundation of Pittsburgh. The Clearing House has four fundamental objectives:

1. To put young citizens with political ambitions in touch with 'an honest and intelligent leader of their own party in their own community.' (Although Justice Vanderbilt is a prominent Republican, his interests are nonpartisan and extend equally to the Democratic and Republican parties.)

2. To form discussion groups in local communities among able and sincere young people, 'regardless of party,' to consider city, state, national, and international problems. 'One of the great losses which we have suffered with the advent of the movies and radio,' says Justice Vanderbilt, 'has been the loss of the art of discussion.'

3. To collect pertinent materials from all parts of the country for use in the teaching of practical politics.

4. To refer promising and zealous young citizens to the best available sources of information on all topics, so they can approach the major political, economic, and social questions of our age with information rather than prejudices.

Some of these functions may seem rather vague. Yet the one active contact my wife and I have had with the program of the Citizenship Clearing House has been, in our estimation, uniquely useful.

At various colleges throughout the land, the Clearing House assembled teachers of political science. From near-by localities were brought mayors, congressmen, campaign managers, officials of political parties, and state legislators like my wife and me. We ate together, talked together, walked together, and even played golf and took in football games together.

We politicians were fair game for the political scientists. They could ask us any question and we were expected to give an honest and complete answer—no hiding behind legislative immunity, the Fifth Amendment, or just plain reticence.

In turn, the political science teachers were expected to go home to their respective schools and tell students the facts of life about American politics. When the party boss cracks the whip, must legislators pull obediently in the traces? Does raising a big campaign treasury end a candidate's independence?

All this might challenge the most vigorous and courageous students to try to make politics better. Still more important, it might prepare them psychologically for what they actually would encounter when they themselves sought elective office. Many idealists, I fear, become discouraged the instant they bump into the stern realities of modern competition at the ballot box. The game of power is a grubby one. It will not be moral and ethical until many upright people have endured the game as it is, and cleaned it up. Gethsemane is frequently the lot of the reformer who would make future betrayals and injustice impossible.

'The preparation of graduates for participation in public life would seem to be a chief reason for the existence of colleges in a democracy,' Arthur Vanderbilt has said.

And a professor at a college in the state of Washington substantially echoed these words when he said to Maurine and me: 'What you have told us about the real happenings in a state legislature is sure to help me induce some of my best students to run for the Washington Senate and House at the next election. I'm not going to be content any more to let these educated and honest young people sit by as mere spectators while uninformed ignoramuses, some of dubious character, dominate contests for positions in our state government.'

II

From our own experience in the legislature of a typical state of the Union, my wife and I are convinced that Justice Vanderbilt is probing at one of the basic problems facing the nation.

The government may decide whether we go to war, what kind of public schools our children attend, the condition of our business and agricultural economy, even the preservation of the resources on which we rely for sustenance and livelihood. Yet the bulk of our citizens feel neither the desire nor the duty to participate in government. This is something left for the other fellow to do. All too often 'the other fellow' turns out to be a person who should not be controlling our destiny in the legislature, congress, or city hall.

I have sat around the fireside while my friends told of

the hopes for their sons. They wanted their sons to be doctors or farmers or pastors or bakers or mechanics. This was well and good. Finally, a merchant said unconcernedly that he trusted his son would decide to go into politics. There was a titter in the corner of the room. Several people looked embarrassed. A hiatus occurred in the conversation. It was obvious that the merchant's remark had evoked consternation and sympathy. The others felt the son of the storekeeper was bound for politics and thus, perhaps, for perdition. Yet the merchant's son, if he attained his goal, might thrust the other sons into uniform, tax them into bankruptcy, or blunder them into an economic depression.

The episode was fresh evidence of the fact that 69 per cent of Americans have indicated they definitely do not want their children to be politicians.

Several reasons probably account for this. Politics promises scant financial reward to the honest citizen, and we live in a society where money has been too much enthroned. Ben Jonson may have expressed the advice still given to many youths when he wrote three centuries ago, 'Get money! Get money, boy, no matter by what means!'

There are rich men in politics, but most of them had well-filled exchequers before they put their names on the ballot. A few wealthy politicians with no other visible means of support only convince the average voter that politics and iniquity are synonymous. But the honest man who has spent a lifetime serving the American public rarely leaves a large estate. The legacy bequeathed by the beloved Senator George W. Norris, after almost 40 years in Congress, was extremely modest. Fred M. Vinson had occupied some of the most exalted positions within the gift of the people, including that of Chief Justice of the United States, but *The New York Times* reported him as leaving only 'an estimated $1000 to his heirs.'

I remember a luncheon with one of the most brilliant young lawyers in our community. I sat between him and the minister of his church. We were trying to convince the young lawyer that he should run for the State Senate. His election, we felt, would be a foregone conclusion. His capacity for effective public service, in our opinion, was equally certain. Yet at length he said to the churchman and to me:

'I'd like to do it but I just can't interrupt my career. I know it would cost me some clients to be away at the legislature for three or four months every two years. I can't afford that kind of slice in my income at a time when I'm attempting to build an estate and lay away some financial security for my wife and children.'

The minister and I looked at each other and shrugged hopelessly. To that argument there was little we could say, particularly when legislative pay in Oregon was so trifling.

But other factors besides finances discourage capable and honest young men and women from entering politics. There is a feeling abroad in the land that politics is not quite respectable, that it is something which people of probity just don't go in for.

In England and Canada, points out Justice Vanderbilt, 'educated people have had a special sense of responsibility for government.' A family takes great pride in the fact that one of its sons or daughters has tried for a seat in Parliament. This responsibility, unfortunately, has been lacking in the United States. Some years ago

Fortune reviewed the careers of 67,000 graduates of the country's twelve leading preparatory schools. A striking feature of the survey was the comparatively few political figures which this large number of graduates had produced.

In American politics a kind of Gresham's Law seems to operate. Just as bad money tends to drive out good money, so do bungling and dishonest politicians act to keep better men from challenging their sovereignty. 'A plague o' both your houses,' comments the average citizen when he watches a bizarre spectacle of corruption, inefficiency, and character assassination. And so this average citizen discourages his own children from going into politics.

On one of my writing trips to Canada, I met a prairie family of four brothers which boasted that it set aside a certain amount of money each month to make it possible for one of the brothers to sit in the House of Commons at Ottawa. Without this assistance, the brother in politics could not have served as an MP for $6000 a year. The other brothers—even those of a different political party—believed they were performing a patriotic duty in enabling their kinsman to be a member of Parliament.

In the United States, by contrast, a man willing to endure the jibes and epithets of politics often gets kicked for his pains. I recall the young bank teller in an Oregon town who had been advised by his boss not to run for the legislature. 'He's afraid my stand on controversial issues might offend some important depositors,' said the teller. 'If I decide to file for the legislature, I'd have to quit my job. I doubt if I can afford to do that. My wife's expecting a baby in two or three months.'

So the young banker did not put his name on the ballot. I doubt now if he ever will. He has risen a notch or two in the bank's echelons. He has still more to lose by risking the enmities and rivalries of politics. His community and his state are the sufferers, for he has the intelligence and integrity to be a first-rate legislator.

The penalties of political participation can be many. I shall never forget the local newspaperman who wrote a review of one of my books for the editorial page of his paper and then had it 'killed' by his editor.

'Why wasn't my book ever reviewed?' I asked him.

'My editor doesn't like your politics,' he replied.

'What has that got to do with a book entitled *The Lewis and Clark Expedition*? Lewis and Clark were explorers. They weren't in politics.'

'And if you hadn't been in politics,' the newspaperman answered, 'your book would have been reviewed on our editorial page.'

Although all of us pay a certain lip-service to the desirability of political service by able young people, this tradition is honored far more in the breach than in the observance.

Near my wife during one session in Oregon's House of Representatives sat an idealistic thirty-six-year-old man, the father of three small children. He was in the haberdashery business in a prosperous farming community. Despite the fact that he was a Republican and we are Democrats, he became one of our close friends. We considered him one of the outstanding members of the legislature, a man who always put personal ethics and convictions above political expediency. Yet he did not file for re-election. His first term in the legislature was also his last. We asked him why.

'I'm in business,' said he. 'I have to make that business a success, because my first responsibility is to my wife and children. But every time I cast a vote on a major issue in the legislature, I lost customers. One side or another would boycott my store and take their trade elsewhere. I couldn't stand that for long. Soon I would have the whole town indignant at me. Nor could I cast an independent vote in the legislature if I had to think each time of the impact on the cash register at home. I decided the one possible solution was to withdraw from politics.'

And so the people of this man's town had lost a fine legislator because they allowed political vindictiveness to reach the stage of economic reprisals against a legislator's livelihood.

This was when Maurine and I decided that a Citizenship Clearing House was necessary not only to encourage 'better' men and women to participate directly in politics, but to educate the general run of citizens in the care and feeding of bright young politicians.

III

'The greatest obstacle to active participation in politics," declares Justice Vanderbilt, 'is the attitude of people generally toward government: "Politics is a dirty game and I don't want my son to enter politics." '

People shut their minds to the call of the ballot. Only 59 per cent of the eligible adults even vote in a national election. Arthur Vanderbilt discovered that a bare 2 per cent of the attendants at a vast political meeting in Montclair, New Jersey, could name their own State Senators, Assemblymen, and County Freeholders. A substantial portion of my constituents think the legislature is in session the year around, rather than a mere four months out of every twenty-four. Most of my mail is sent to the state capital instead of to my home community.

Yet the American people are not indifferent to the other responsibilities of citizenship. I have seen soldiers from the balmy South slogging through stunted spruce forests to build the Alcan Highway in cruel temperatures of 60° below zero. Other soldiers fought valorously against the *Reichswehr* in Normandy and against the Communist aggressors in Korea. Yet these same soldiers, on discharge from the armed services, have seemed to flinch from the verbal missiles of politics. This is an anomaly. Justice Vanderbilt has pointed out many times that political brickbats, despite their unpleasantness, 'are a small price to pay when compared with what the citizen-soldier has been called upon to endure in war.'

Tangible results of the Citizenship Clearing House program are starting to be visible. The young secretary of Rutgers University has just been elected Mayor of Metuchen, New Jersey, in a candid test of whether the people will vote for a confessed political 'amateur.' Citizens for Eisenhower and Volunteers for Stevenson were composed of newcomers to politics who conspicuously shunned the old-line party organizations. A philanthropic woman, Elizabeth C. Ducey, has given a generous financial grant to Reed College in Oregon 'for the purpose of exploring ways in which the study of politics can be made more relevant to the living process and to real and concrete situations.'

In the churches, too, there is an increasing awareness of the need for participation in politics by young men and women of religious background and educational at-

tainments. Once I was asked to church suppers and so-
cials in our community only to talk about my books. Indeed, I was cautioned not to venture the most gingerly
political opinion. Today this has been reversed. Church
groups invite me specifically to discuss burning issues of
politics. The local Methodist Men's Club kept me nearly
to midnight discussing the question of public or private
power development at Hell's Canyon on the Snake
River.

Afterward, the Reverend Laurence Nye said to me, 'I
notice some change in the attitude of our members
toward politics. They still get fed up on the antics of
politicians. But they are becoming increasingly aware
of the urgent need for better politicians. I believe we
are going to get a much better participation in American politics before very many more years go by.'

Some promising young people never enter active politics, I am convinced, because they have not mastered the
simple mechanics of it. What do they do? Where do they
go? How do they start? Who tells them their duties and
obligations? How can they avoid getting into the wrong
hands?

People, even brave people, are often essentially timid
about any undertaking that involves social finesse. Politics throws many bright young men and women for an
opening loss, because politics is complicated. You don't
become a precinct committeeman or file for the legislature as simply as you open a bank account or buy a sec-
ondhand car.

This is why one of the principal aims of the Citizenship Clearing House is so important: 'to introduce college students to honest, intelligent leaders of their own
political party, each in his or her own town. . .'

Today we wonder why some young participants in politics fall into association with racketeers or with Communist fellow-travelers. I believe these connections frequently begin in total innocence, simply because the embryo politician is as hapless as the embryo stage actor or movie starlet who takes up with bad companions. By enabling young men and women of promise to start under the proper political auspices, the Citizenship Clearing House will more than fulfill its mission. There are devoted idealists in both major political parties, but not enough beginners receive their active attention and sponsorship.

This is why the Citizenship Clearing House is paying special heed to teachers of political science in various parts of the country. If these teachers can become acquainted with the better people in local politics, they can guide their students accordingly. No longer need the teachers give shotgun advice to get into politics, any old way. They can point with rifle-like accuracy to 'X' in the Republican Party or 'Y' in the Democratic organization. 'Go and see him. He will advise you what to do. He is worthy of your trust.'

State Legislatures are the logical place for political careers to commence, so the program of the Citizenship Clearing House is particularly important to state government. 'Better minds for better politics' is sure to pay off first at the state level. Like Jefferson and Lincoln and the two Roosevelts, the average young person of zeal and courage will decide to walk politically before he tries to run. The legislature is the best place to test his electoral legs at a modest gait.

'We don't want Federal domination of the people,'

said Dwight D. Eisenhower in the 1952 campaign. 'The states must play a leading role in government.'

But what if the best minds and the most honest hearts think it is preferable to be a butcher or baker or candle-stickmaker than to be a State legislator? Can the states then fulfill the President's high hopes? The Citizenship Clearing House offers one of the real possibilities for making 'states' rights' something besides a political slogan to be refurbished every four years.

– 5 –

TWO-PARTY BLUES

IN A ONE-PARTY STATE

I

People often come and stare at us. Others ask for our autographs. One or two even snap our pictures for their albums. A few avoid us ostentatiously. No wonder my wife and I feel like animals at the zoo on Sunday.

Why are we such rare specimens?

We are Democrats elected in Republican Oregon, where Democrats make up a mere 15 per cent of the total membership of the legislature, and my wife and I comprise exactly 15 per cent of that puny 15 per cent. Doorkeepers in the galleries of the State Senate and House tell my wife and me that visitors ask to have us pointed out more often than any other members. After all, some Oregon counties have not sent a Democrat to the State capital since the railroads crossed the Great Divide!

Folks frequently seem surprised to discover that we are human—that if we are pricked, we bleed. A while back my wife spoke at a tea given by a former group in

a small town along the timbered Oregon seacoast. A
gray-haired lady surveyed Maurine from leather pumps
to Mamie-style bangs. This critical examination went
on for a minute or so. Then the woman said to my
wife:

'Well, I declare! You don't look very much different
from the rest of us!'

'How did you expect me to look?' asked my wife.

'I wouldn't really know,' replied the woman. 'I never
saw a lady Democrat before. I had an idea, though,
that there'd be something about you that was kind
of funny or abnormal.'

We frequently are asked what it is like to be part of
a legislative minority so small that it is not physically
possible to have our own side of the aisle. Can a legislative chamber be so lopsidedly divided, 85 per cent on
one side of the separating corridor, 15 per cent on the
other?

A few hardy souls in other states surely must share
our adventures to some degree. This nation contains
more one party states than most Americans realize; in
twenty, for example, one party is a permanent minority
so weak that it seldom wins more than 20 per cent of
the seats in the Legislature. Most of the twenty lie in
the Democratic South, but there are numerous Republican fortresses too, including Iowa, Kansas, South Dakota, Maine, and Vermont as well as Oregon.

Oregon's most recent Democratic United States Senator was elected in 1914. The last Democratic Legislature
sat in 1878. Of the ten past Governors of Oregon, eight
have been Republicans.

A strange double-standard threads through the life
of a one-party state. In Portland, the city where we live,

municipal government is nonpartisan. This means, of course, that we are governed by a City Council of five members, all of them Republicans. When a Democrat filed for Mayor, he was accused of partisanship.

With thirteen House seats to be filled in the county, the *Oregonian* editorial page has been known to decide solemnly that all thirteen Republicans are vastly superior to the thirteen Democratic nominees. Signboards between the two parties are divided in the ratio of approximately 1000 to 1. Indeed, this may even be an understatement. Rarely does a Democrat have any outdoor advertising. Republican names, by contrast, are plastered about like the nationally advertised products.

When my wife was on the board of the local League of Women Voters, someone nervously brought up the fact that she was a Democratic precinct committeewoman. This was contrary to the impartial principles of the league, which is one of the community's most useful organizations.

My wife smiled sweetly across the table at the objector. 'Aren't you a Republican precinct committeewoman, Frances?' she asked.

'Well, yes,' admitted Frances, 'but I don't think that's exactly the same thing.'

The board of the league hurriedly moved on to the next order of business.

If you are a Democrat in our state, suspicion sticks to you like mucilage. People try their level best to be nice and agreeable, but somehow the feeling persists that you don't quite belong.

I was pleased with an invitation to be the main speaker at a large civic banquet in a city on the high upland desert. To my astonishment, another orator shared the head table. He was to address the gathering after I was through. I knew the toastmaster was tense and jittery. He finally blurted out the reason for this double billing.

'Some of our people found out you were a Democrat,' said he. 'They felt we had to have a Republican to wind up the program, to correct any misinformation you might possibly give the audience.'

II

But not all the aspects of the one-party state are humorous. Some are tragic, with somber results for the people who live in the state.

A white-haired man came to my desk in the Senate. He was obviously under great tension. His hands trembled and his eyes were watery. I did not know then that Nels Rogers, Oregon's State Forester, was dying of Hodgkin's disease. He handed me four plats showing the cruise reports made by his men of state school timber in the vicinity of Lookout Mountain. The foresters had turned in a specific and unequivocal recommendation: 'Timber should be sold by oral auction, preferably at Bend, Oregon, with considerable advance publicity and advertising. The appraised stumpage price and minimum acceptable should be about $20 per thousand board-feet. The land should be retained by the state.'

No part of the recommendation had been followed by the Republican-dominated State Land Board. The school timber had been sold at a private proceeding in Salem. The price accepted had been less than that advised by the cruise report. The land had gone along with the trees of yellow pine. The fortunate buyer had been represented by one of Oregon's highest-ranking Republican lawyers.

What happened? Because Oregon is a one-party state, nothing happened. The Republican legislature viewed the affair placidly. Inasmuch as legislative committees had authority neither to take testimony under oath nor to subpoena witnesses, the handful of Democratic members could do nothing to bring the participants to book. The major newspapers in the state of Oregon did not look up from their berating of Democratic sins in Washington, D. C., to take editorial notice of this Republican mishandling of the timber that was the legacy of Oregon's school children.

Nels Rogers, since dead, was a Republican appointee of a Republican state regime. But his first obligation was to forestry, his profession, and to the school timber in his care. Yet he, too, was crushed by the suffocating quilt of one-party politics. There existed no rival political party of strength to which he could take his tale of this outrage against the school children of Oregon, to whom the timber belonged. Eighty per cent of the state's press was committed to continued Republican sovereignty. Could it spread Rogers' story? It is characteristic of some one-party states that the newspapers mold their consciences to the morals of the dominant political group. The king can do no wrong! In Oregon only a few dailies defy this crushing pressure.

The looting of Oregon's school timber, a process of pillage extending over many generations, explains why many of us in the Pacific Northwest are opposed to the Congressional decision of turning over the oil deposits under the marginal seas to the states—in this instance actually four states, where the reserves are located.

In spite of the concessions made to special interests by the Eisenhower administration, the Federal government is still a more vigilant custodian of resources than are most of the states. McKay and his confederates have not been able to quench completely the spirit of Pinchot and Ickes. To begin with, bona fide competition between the political parties generally prevails at the Federal level. This keeps the party in power closer to the straight and narrow. It never can tell when the minority may seize some issue which will transpose positions between minority and majority. But in nearly half the states, the dominant party feels no sense of peril. What if it is careless with the people's heritage? The next election is sure to be just like the last election.

The contrast in protection of school lands is striking in the Northwest. Oregon has been a one-party state during much of its history. The state of Washington, however, has been an arena of greater political competition. Both states, when they were admitted to the Union, received sections 16 and 36 of each township 'for school purposes.' These sections fell on some of the finest Douglas fir and Ponderosa pine timber ever to thrust needled boughs toward Heaven. Here is the school-land record of the two states:

	OREGON	WASHINGTON
Acres received	4,203,000	2,298,000
Acres still in trust for schools	765,000	1,756,000
Funds in permanent school account from use of lands	$10,771,000	$49,318,000

Oregon's shabby handling of school timber underscores why so many conservationists consider the national government the best available guardian of natural resources. U. S. Forest Rangers, protected by civil service, have more freedom to live up to their calling than do state employees in similar roles. My experience with the lower echelon of state officials and bureaucrats has been favorable. They are, for the most part, honest and conscientious. But in many states they are politically vulnerable, because the dominant party can behave about as it wishes, without fear of retribution at the polls.

In the one-party states, if Oregon can be considered as typical, great immaturity exists regarding normal political rivalry. Democrats hardly are looked upon as members of the clan *homo sapiens*. After my wife filed for the legislature on the Democratic ticket, several scheduled speaking engagements were canceled because she was participating in 'partisan politics.' A Republican running for Congress later appeared before some of the same groups. Presumably he was not in 'partisan politics.'

A Democrat missed many meetings of the legislature because of unsuccessful bouts with John Barleycorn. Newspapers called attention to his frequent absences and hinted at the reason. A prominent Republican was away from even more legislative meetings and because of a similar weakness. The papers were silent.

All of this, of course, is childish and superficial. Yet it corrodes state government and tells why the Federal government has had to take over in so many important realms of activity. Without competition, the party in power is not on its mettle. Furthermore, state government is rarely exposed to the kind of investigations which occasionally get at fundamental faults in the Federal structure.

If any dereliction occurs in Oregon's state government, it probably will not be probed by the legislature. During our service in the legislative assembly, we never have seen any agency actually examined and analyzed by the legislature. Should criminal doings be suspected, a grand jury working under a Republican district attorney might possibly take a peek. But it is all a cozy arrangement, with one party safely in control.

Some of this, obviously, is the fault of us Democrats. We have provided an ineffective opposition or we might have ended the one-party hegemony. Yet an iron ring surrounds us—a ring consisting of Republican newspapers, Republican courthouses, Republican state agencies, and Republican domination of political campaign funds. Once we could crack the ring, these battlements might fall. But which comes first? Can we break out of the circle before we overcome some of the odds?

Indeed, the Republicans have so little fear of us as a political force that a few of the Democrats in the legislature are given important committee chairmanships. Naturally, we are well hemmed in. I preside over a Senate Elections Committee consisting of one Democrat and six Republicans. Maurine heads a House Education Committee made up of two Democrats and eight Republicans.

Several of my friends on the political science teaching staff at Oregon State College think we would be well-advised to foresake these crumbs and to fight a little harder for the whole loaf. They believe the Democratic legislative minority, regardless of its infinitesimal dimensions, should put up its own candidates for Speaker of the House and President of the Senate. We do not do this now because of our paucity in numbers. These counselors warn that we never will achieve majority status until we carry out the obligations and duties of a courageous minority.

With each passing political episode, I become more convinced they are right. In Oregon we have seen the truth of Tocqueville's warning: 'In the United States, as soon as a party has become preponderant, all the public authority passes under its control. Its private supporters occupy all the places, and have all the force of the administration at their disposal.' This is more prevalent in one-party states than in the nation as a whole, where the political balance is closer. We shall try in Oregon to remove at least one political monopoly from the list which has weakened the effectiveness of state government in America.

III

No one who likes to play it high, wide, and handsome should ever join the minority party in a one-party state like Oregon. We are the permanent poor relations of Oregon politics. Big contributors are sure we have no chance to win, and so they rarely open their wallets in our presence.

In 1948 the Republican party in the state spent $211,-071. We Oregon Democrats didn't have quite this much to spend. Our total was $1025. In 1952 we did much better vis-à-vis our Republican opponents. They spent $315,400, but we Democrats managed to collect $29,800. This was the best we ever did financially. Our party headquarters had a telephone, and the company even left it hooked up until Election Day. We were able to complete payments on the mimeograph machine.

The Republicans regard us paternally. It is true that we pester them occasionally by winning a seat or two in the Legislature or grabbing off a sheriff's job. But they seem content with a legislative majority like the 75-to-15 edge they enjoy at present.

How does even a handful of Democrats manage to get elected in this one-party state? Certainly not by an attitude of 'my party, right or wrong.'

My wife and I, for example, are lucky enough to be fairly well known in the state—she as a teacher of English and modern dance, I as a writer. Furthermore, we are not regarded as rabid Democratic partisans either. Although we both spoke and debated on many occasions for Adlai Stevenson, my wife helped lead the campaign of a prominent Republican woman for mayor. I denounced some of my fellow State Senate Democrats in 1951 for backing a teachers' loyalty oath and, conversely, gave credit for its defeat to an ex-Republican Governor, Charles Sprague, who opposed the idea in his newspaper, the *Salem Statesman*.

These things brought down upon us Democratic wrath, but evidently made our preponderantly Republican constituents feel that party garments fitted us only loosely. Yet, in general, we support the Democratic philosophy. Both of us have delivered many speeches assailing the efforts of the Republican Secretary of the Interior to abandon public power on the Columbia River. We regard the desertion of the Hell's Canyon dam site by Oregon's ex-Governor, Douglas McKay, as a high crime against an orderly program of conservation in the Northwest. It gives us a feeling of exhilaration to work in such great causes.

Nevertheless, to be enrolled in a pygmy legislative minority is to have a feeling of helplessness, like trying to swim up Victoria Falls.

Four years ago I began pioneering for a constitutional convention to revise Oregon's outdated and cluttered basic charter. My bills could not get out of committee. They were pigeonholed summarily. I was denounced as a heretic for suggesting that the Constitution needed a face-lifting.

Now our Republican Governor has endorsed the idea in his inaugural message—and designated a Republican to sponsor the bill I originally drafted. I am not to be allowed to have a part in the adoption of my own idea!

Often we are asked why we persist in being Democrats in a realm where Democrats face so fierce a struggle for survival. We are suspected of masochism, of political self-torture. The example of Oregon's maverick United States Senator, Wayne L. Morse, frequently is pointed out. People claim that Morse, like us, is a Democrat at heart. But he had to be at least a nominal Republican to get safely across the tundra at election time in one-party Oregon, although he now has proclaimed his status as an Independent.

Evidently martyrdom suits our personalities. Maurine and I enjoy being caribou in timber-wolf terrain. It gives us a sense of high adventure and derring-do.

Occasionally we even force our colleagues to pass a bill or two. Their fondest ambition is to keep on being in a lopsided majority. If the Neubergers come up with a good idea, some of the Republicans believe discretion is the better part of valor. They put the idea on the statute books. Of course, they first try to take our names off the bill. This was why Maurine's baby-sitting tax deduction became part of an omnibus tax measure. In that way a Democratic name could be easily omitted. Republicans even might go home and proclaim, 'We did it!'

Life in a one-party state makes evident that political principles rarely are allowed to interfere with the winning of elections. During the campaign of 1952 the Republicans in Oregon made a considerable show of deploring 'twenty long years of Democratic rule in Washington, D. C.' We heard again and again General Eisenhower's claim that unbroken political tenure for one party resulted in corruption, waste, and inefficiency.

Quite naturally, we reminded our Republican friends that they had not lost control of the Oregon Legislature since 1878, and that this interval of seventy-four years exceeded by nearly four times the reign of the Democrats in the national capital.

The Republicans had a ready answer for us, when confronted with the chronological record of their one-party monopoly at the state level. 'Ah,' said they. 'But that's different!'

One must have a sense of humor to be in the perennial minority in a one-party state. A Republican colleague in the Senate said Mrs. Neuberger and I had nothing to complain about, despite our low-on-the-totem-pole status. He called my attention to the fact that a minority Senator in the French West African Parliament had recently been eaten by his constituents. 'Be thankful,' adjured my legislative friend, 'that we Oregon Republicans have no cannibalistic tendencies.'

– 6 –

WHERE THOSE FUNNY BILLS

COME FROM

I

ON the day that an atomic blast was touched off at Yucca Flat, Oregon's State Senate debated a bill to forbid installation of television sets in automobiles. We debated it long and strenuously, and finally the bill was passed by a vote of 23 to 7.

On another day, when President Rhee in distant Korea was hinting that he had an itchy trigger finger, we wrangled over a bill denying movie theaters the right to sell popcorn and peanuts in the lobby. The sponsor of the bill told us that the grinding of patrons' teeth on these crunchy tidbits kept other viewers from hearing the sound track.

The sessions of our forty-eight state legislatures frequently show that this attention to mundane and often trivial things is characteristic of local lawmakers. Congress may discuss billion-dollar appropriations, standby price controls, and even war or peace for all mankind. But the typical state legislature is preoccupied with

83

matters far closer to home—measures like Oregon House
Bill 363, which makes a fisherman guilty of a misdemeanor if he leaves his rod and line untended to go off
on an errand.

Trifling as these matters are, compared to such global questions as the North Atlantic Treaty Alliance or
who shall man our vital listening post in Moscow, they
are of burning significance in our state, where people
can get more worked up about a bill forbidding women
bartenders than about the real responsibilities of state
government.

Actually, our Legislature does argue such crucial issues as highway taxes, school reorganization, and control
of expenditures in political campaigns. We set standards
of food sanitation and we frame rules for courts and
persons. We do many important things. Yet the legislative mail pouch frequently gets its biggest bulge not
from these matters but from some bill that may appear
irresponsibly frivolous to the detached observer.

The atmosphere of the typical state capital is geared
to a plodding, unsophisticated pace. As we shall see in
a later chapter, most of these places were established by
frontiersmen who thought they were locating the seat
of government in what would be the biggest city of the
state—but they guessed wrong.

Thus, Maryland's 2,343,000 people look for orders to
Annapolis (pop. 10,047). The 4,000,000 residents of Missouri are governed from Jefferson City (pop. 25,099).
None of the five greatest American cities—New York,
Chicago, Philadelphia, Los Angeles, or Detroit—is a state
capital. Although Portland, Oregon, has 380,000 inhabitants, the turreted state capitol building looms above

The lady legislator shows the Agricultural committee
what housewives had to do to hand-color their margarine.

The husband-and-wife legislative team plans for
the day's meetings in the House of Representatives.

The Neubergers, husband and wife, comprise 15 per cent of the Democratic membership in Oregon's legislature.

Salem of sylvan atmosphere, with a population barely more than a tenth of Portland's.

In these surroundings folks accept in matter-of-fact fashion bills requiring bed sheets in hotels to be long enough to tuck comfortably under a standard-sized mattress. What's so funny about that?

The more localized the measure, the more intense the debate becomes between its supporters and its foes. A terse bill outlawed the operation of motor vehicles on any Oregon beach 'supervised by a lifeguard.' Owners of summer cottages at one resort were outraged over the use of the beach by speeding cars while their children roamed around at bathing time. But the owners of restaurants, filling stations, and grocery stores argued that the hard-packed sands were a lure to thousands of tourists who wanted the thrill of pushing throttles clear to the floorboards with no state trooper in the offing.

This resulted in a longer debate than that over the memorial to Congress urging adoption of the Bricker amendment, which would limit the treaty-making powers of the President of the United States.

Long ago I ceased predicting which bill will keep us from adjournment. One day, when only a single unobtrusive measure remained on our calendar, I began to fasten the zipper on my briefcase. I had decided I would order broiled Chinook salmon for dinner and already I could taste it.

Two hours later I still was squirming hungrily in my seat in the Senate. The bill gave a county sheriff the right to burn and hack off ragweed and then tax the proprietor of the land for the clearing operations. Among my colleagues sat substantial property owners as well as tormented hay-fever sufferers. One hay-fever victim sneezed frequently with a vigor and gusto that ruined the aplomb of colleagues within range.

Rival cries of 'tyranny' and 'humanity' shook the chamber. At last the bill was sent back to committee for burial. The holders of deeds in fee simple had outnumbered the members with red eyes and dripping noses.

Few Americans at one time or another have not proclaimed, 'There ought to be a law!' Legislators—particularly state legislators—are ordinary Americans. Many of the bills smacking of buffoonery actually stem from some individual experience or interest.

A legislator's toes are cold one night at a hotel, and that seems reason enough to write the bill requiring longer bed sheets in all places of public accommodation. He gets painfully stung by a bee, and the result is a hotly debated bill imposing heavy fines on careless apiarists.

In urging adoption of a bill to require a high-school education for barbers, an Oregon Representative with a Phi Beta Kappa key dangling from his watch chain read off a list of barbers' malaprops he had endured, some of which, he believed, were offensive to members of the House. Moreover, he added: 'Barbers who are better educated will be able to inform their customers more adequately on the coming election. I may eventually extend my bill to include taxicab drivers.'

This brought a laugh, although the member may have regretted his humor. The secretary of the Barbers' Union pointed out, and truthfully, that many barbers were a whole lot better informed than the folks whom they served tonsorially.

II

One of our longest and angriest debates in the Oregon Senate concerned a bill, presented primarily as a safety measure, to keep television sets out of automobiles. A burly official of the Teamsters' Union, who occupies the Senate desk next to mine, angrily demanded: 'Why don't you forbid blondes from ever getting into automobiles, too? The lousy programs I've seen on TV wouldn't distract one of my drivers half as much as some cute dish sitting on the seat beside him!'

Occasionally great political cunning lies behind bills which are ostensibly absurd. Some of their sponsors are crazy like foxes. A trivial bill, with humorous or burlesque aspects, may net more attention—and benevolent publicity—than a measure directed at some major problem of government.

Moreover, bills of this sort seldom collect a large assortment of political enemies for their authors. No one swears everlasting retribution at the ballot box if a state Senator introduces a law forbidding 'Bikini' bathing suits beside Oregon lakes—as one of my colleagues did on the ground that they threatened reduction in the use of Oregon wool.

'To heck with the wool market!' exclaimed a young Representative who, needless to add, came from a seacoast area far from the upland meadows where sheep forage.

It was a father's impassioned plea that originally induced Washington's State Senate to authorize blinker lights and sirens on cars owned by legislators.

'I have six small children,' said the Seattle Senator. 'Every time I'm in the downtown area and the Mayor of Seattle zooms by with his siren screaming, my kids ask, "Who's that, Daddy?"

'I tell them that's the Mayor.

' "Well," say my children, "he's only a city official. You're a state official. How come we don't have red lights and a siren on our car?" '

In Oregon a bill came in to do away with the legal first bite now allowed every dog, be it St. Bernard or Pomeranian. The proposals got no attention—for two or three days. Then the legislative postal clerks began to lose their bearings in the blizzard of letters and postcards.

The ratio of dog-lovers to supporters of delivery boys was approximately 50 to 1 in the case of our Senatorial mail, and the bill was locked securely in committee.

As these words are written one of my warm friends in the legislature is still zealously pushing his bill to put license plates of a special color on the cars of persons found guilty of drunken driving.

'But, Joe,' I remonstrated, 'how often do you look at a car's license plates before it bumps into you?'

'I'm afraid you haven't ever read the bill,' said my Legislator friend sternly. 'Right on the first page the bill provides that the special plates for drunken drivers "shall be larger than regular license plates." '

The moral is the next time you laugh over a silly bill, try to remember that your levity probably would shock its author. A past president of the Oregon State Bar Association made front-page news throughout the country with his bill requiring that a hole be filled before it is dug, and vice versa. 'We'll amend it into shape in committee,' he said reassuringly. 'If we had the language to botch it, we have the language to fix it.'

Not all the funny bills are always as funny as they seem. My friend with the plan for special license plates for drunks was thinking of all the whisky-soaked barflies who go out on U. S. 99 or State Highway 50, with two-hundred horsepower at their hazy command. But state legislatures appear concerned with minutiae because we often lack the technical assistance to prepare fundamental bills properly.

It takes a tax expert to draft legislation which will compel out-of-state corporations to pay adequately for their inroads on a state's mineral, timber, or water resources. But anyone with glands and a fountain pen can write one of those funny bills making it a misdemeanor for a female to wear a doll-sized bathing suit on one of Oregon's picturesque public beaches.

- 7 -

STATE CAPITAL—

ANY STATE CAPITAL

I

WHEN Maurine and I sign in for a legislative session, our way of life changes. All at once, we are in a comparatively small community for three or four months. To Maurine it is like going part of the way back home, for she was brought up on an Oregon farm. For me, it is a useful reminder that the metropolis is only one segment of America. We grumble about Salem, and yet I doubt if we would have it differently. Is it so bad that we leave the impersonal atmosphere of the metropolis to dwell among the friendly and inquisitive inhabitants of a prosperous trading center in a lush agricultural hinterland?

Furthermore, we tell ourselves that politicians still would be politicians, even if Salem became New York or London. If they do not use the excellent State Library, would they visit the Museum of Natural History? What attraction can compare with a hotel room, highballs, Swiss cheese on rye—and talk of politics?

When Bennett Cerf spoke in Salem, we counted two other legislators in the audience. Maurine could discern no other members at a performance of a talented ballet company. A scholarly lecture by a State Supreme Court Justice opposing the Bricker amendment attracted Salem townspeople but relatively few lawmakers, who were soon to adopt a memorial urging Congress to add the Bricker amendment to the Constitution of the United States.

Most Americans live in big cities, but their state laws are enacted in places that would fit into the metropolis many times. Furthermore, a majority of the men and women whose *yeas* and *nays* shape these laws come either from even smaller communities or from the rural hinterland.

This has had a profound effect on life in the United States. The Federal government may decide when and where our men go to war, but it is the government of each state that controls schools, courts, colleges, welfare standards, electric light rates, highways, mental institutions, and the criminal code. This is a realm close to every citizen's daily problems.

A few state capitals are in great centers of population. Yet Boston, Denver, Indianapolis, and Atlanta are merely exceptions which confirm the rule. The laws for New York City's 7,835,000 souls are intoned up the Hudson at Albany (pop. 134,000). The crowded millions of Philadelphia toe the mark when the legislature meets in Harrisburg, a place of 89,000. Louisville, with its 370,000 residents, looks for orders to a community of less than 12,000, Frankfort.

It is a salutary thing, in many respects, that San Francisco and Los Angeles, which dominate California financially and economically, must be beholden for statutory commands to Sacramento, with a negligible 6 per cent of Los Angeles' population. And although Seattle has swollen to 500,000, its mayor and council go hats in hand to Olympia (pop. 15,711) for permission to install parking meters or operate municipal parking lots.

Is it good or is it bad that the laws which govern us the most intimately should be considered in a preponderantly rural atmosphere?

It could be both. Perhaps the countryside should lay a restraining hand on the city. As we get ever farther from our frontier origins, more and more Americans are crowded into skyscraper apartment houses or stereotyped by monotonous subdivisions. Rural influence may be responsible for the only individuality we retain. But should not the inhabitants of the city exercise control over their own destinies?

The legislature in which my wife and I serve is in many ways typical of Salem, the city where the legislature sits. Salem has 50,00 inhabitants. It is not a metropolis; neither is it the backwoods. It rejected a Renoir statue of Venus because Venus was nude. Yet Salem has a fine school system, it generously patronizes visiting orchestras and theatrical troupes, and its *Statesman* is far superior to the average small-town daily.

The Oregon legislature is friendly, cautious, well meaning, slow-moving, preponderantly honest, and deplorably uninformed on many basic issues. A proposed memorial denouncing a past Secretary of State spelled his name as 'Atchison' and several days passed before the error was detected. Although my wife and I are Democrats, our colleagues seem to like us personally. There are more dinner invitations than we can accept.

Yet other members are suspicious when we suggest the legislature should be unicameral in form or that the lobbyists who buy steaks, liquor, and entertainment should register and reveal the sources of their financing. The atmosphere is clubby, and I got hard stares from my fellows when I proposed that smoking be forbidden during formal debate.

By solemn legislative enactment, each member can subscribe to five papers at state expense. When, in addition to the Portland dailies, my wife took the *New York Herald Tribune* and *Denver Post* and I put in for *The New York Times* and *St. Louis Post-Dispatch,* those around us on the floor of House and Senate were astonished. They asked if a mistake had been made. None of them could understand going so far afield, although I noticed that my *Times* began to be well dog-eared after a few weeks had passed and the innovation no longer was a nine days' wonder.

Whatever the atmosphere of the capital, the men and women who make the laws never forget that hinterland constituency which sent them there. It may be distant and unseen, yet it is omnipresent.

Whatever their prevailing politics, state capitals are invariably pleasant places. Majestic buildings probably contribute to this congenial atmosphere. I have never been in a state capital which did not seem far more appealing than the average small town in America. A sense of history undoubtedly is an added factor. Big things once happened here. Big things are likely to happen again. Wholly apart from my admiration for Adlai Stevenson, I would say that Springfield, Illinois, embodies this zest and anticipation to a high degree.

Springfield lies in the heart of what local people call

'the Lincoln country.' Lincoln's colonial residence is just one attraction. Seventeen miles away is the model village of New Salem, maintained as an Illinois state park. It is an exact replica, log for log, trundle bed for trundle bed, of the lonely settlement in which Lincoln worked as a young storekeeper. And on the edge of Springfield is the memorable tomb of the sixteenth President.

State capitals are as varied as people, but every capital offers something unique. Travel bureaus report that visitors from Europe, in particular, are astonished to discover that a capital is rarely the largest city of its state. This is contrary to the Continental tradition. In Europe the great place is the capital—London, Paris, Rome, Berlin, Stockholm. This even is true of the provincial capitals of neighboring Canada. Teeming Winnipeg is the seat of government for vast Manitoba. Lonely and gaunt Alberta is governed from Edmonton, fastest-growing city on the continent.

When legislatures are in session capital cities have an added attraction for the wayfarer. While the Oregon State Assembly is in session at Salem, in the heart of the fertile Willamette river valley, busses bring tours from every county to see Oregon's policy-making body at work. The Senator or Representative whose home folks are in the gallery then introduces them in a body. They rise somewhat self-consciously and are lustily applauded by the solons at their desks. This occurs in practically all the Western states, where the capital generally is located in a comparatively small city somewhat distant from the principal metropolis.

In addition to being the citadel of authority and power, many state capitals in the West are centers of recreation and outdoor beauty. Olympia, Washington, lies at the extreme lower end of Puget Sound, midway between the white battlements of the Olympic Range and the long-extinct volcanic peaks of the Cascades. On a bright day the state's legislators, strolling out of their carpeted chambers, can see the lordly 14,408-foot summit of Mount Rainier to the east and the snow-tipped crown of Mount Olympus in the west. Paved roads lead from Olympia to the foothills of both mountains. If I were asked to name the most scenically located seat of government in North America, I would be torn between Olympia and Victoria, the island capital of the province of British Columbia—and both are in the same general area of fir trees, salt water, and icy mountains. They are satellites of Puget Sound.

Gubernatorial mansions are another source of attraction for tourists. The downstairs floors of these official residences are generally open to visitors at specified hours. Washington has a particularly inviting home for its chief executives because the windows command a panorama of the long arm of Puget Sound, extending northward to Tacoma and Seattle. When the luxurious residence is accessible to tourists, the silver service from the old *U. S. S. Washington* and other historic relics are put on display.

Most state capitol buildings have guides on duty, regardless of whether the legislature is on the scene. In Oregon's modernistic capitol a continuing source of interest is the huge panel of murals showing such memorable events as the arrival of the Lewis and Clark expedition and the forming of a new constitution. School children are brought in caravans from all over the state to see the building from which Oregon is governed.

The guides report that European visitors often linger longer in the capitol than do those from elsewhere in the United States.

Another tourist loadstone of special interest is the Nebraska state capitol at Lincoln, possibly because many visitors know it to be the only governmental citadel in the nation with a one-house legislature. Attendants at Lincoln say that curiosity about the state assembly has increased since it departed from the orthodox two-chamber legislature to become unicameral in form.

Even in distant Alaska, the seat of government is a prime tourist lure. Cruise ships of the Canadian Pacific, Canadian National, and Alaska Lines stop long enough in Juneau for passengers to pass through the Territorial Capitol building and to visit the high-roofed mansion of the Governor, a residence that blends colonial pillars with a tall frowning totem pole of the Tsimshean Indian tribe. Of course, my own personal predilection for Juneau has increased since enlightened voters sent some Indians and Eskimos to speak for them in the old brownstone office building where Alaska's Territorial laws are made.

II

Oregon, in common with nearly all other western states, allows its people to lose a substantial sum of money annually at racetracks. The state's modest share of the racing 'take' goes not into the General Fund but is apportioned among the thirty-six county fairs. This, in turn, makes each fair board and 4-H Club a lobbying organization for the tracks. In California the Santa Anita horse races help shore up children's homes, polio drives, and other charities.

In Salem, Charles A. Sprague, ex-Republican Governor and a journalistic figure comparable in our territory to William Allen White, let loose a blast. His column in the *Statesman* claimed this system was degrading. The county fairs, he said, were being bribed to lend their political support to the racetracks.

The next day I was talking to a Republican legislator from the wide open spaces in the Senate lounge. 'Sprague's right as rain, of course,' he admitted, 'but I can't possibly vote that way.'

And the Senator added: 'You see, the *Statesman* never gets to my district. My voters don't read Sprague's pieces. But they rub elbows every day with the county fair folks who want that money from the racetracks. I'd be a gone goose politically if I cast a vote here at the capital the way Governor Sprague wants me to.'

To those of us from Portland, the metropolis of the state, Salem, is a small place. But to Senators and Representatives from the backwoods, and they are legion, Salem is quite a city. They revel in its pleasures and confide that four months in Salem every other year is one of the tangible rewards of election. It is the members from the metropolis who are most likely to arrive at the legislature without their wives. But to a wife from an apple orchard or rural crossroads, the legislature is an event not to be passed up.

I have seen lumbermen and cattle ranchers who drove up in shiny Cadillacs or Lincolns and yet had their wives beside them on the floor of the chamber as clerks at $10 a day. The answer wasn't necessarily penuriousness. The wife just didn't want to miss a trick. She was going to be right at her man's elbow with Thesaurus and the

Information Please Almanac when he tangled oratorically with the slicker from the big city.

More than half our members have their wives on the House or Senate payroll, although a political writer for the *Oregonian* made an offhand estimate of the income of the average legislator to be at least $10,000 a year.

The majestic Senator Borah of Idaho remarked to me in 1936 that a state legislature was somewhat like a minor league baseball club—'full of has-been's or would-be's.' Few legislatures would fail to bear him out.

Our ornate chamber is about equally divided between the young eager-beavers who feel they are on the threshold of glory and the old, tired political warhorses who have never quite attained it. Most of the young hopefuls are operating on schedules as split-second as that of the Twentieth Century Limited. Each knows exactly when the legislature will have sufficiently served his purpose to make possible a bid for Congress, the governorship, or the U. S. Senate. And to keep him on his mettle, he usually sits amidst old-timers who grabbed for the mace at the wrong time and now must be content with this modest political pittance. We find the old-timers considerably more human and bearable.

There are no secrets in a compact little group like ours, where lack of office space compels every member except the presiding officer to answer his correspondence and prepare his bills right on the open floor. We all know who is angling for the seat in the Second Congressional District and who will be forever frustrated because the Senator from the next desk beat him to the gubernatorial chamber. And inasmuch as politics is a cruel game, these matters are alluded to and often within earshot of the victim.

Personal lives are even more poorly concealed, and legislators treading the primrose path find this is likely to be better known in the marble rotunda of the capitol than are the roll calls on the bills they are sponsoring. Careful measurement also is made of alcoholic intake. A man who has imbibed generously the night before will be regarded as easy prey in the morning debate. Bloodshot eyes generally invite oratorical barbs.

Despite the fact that in the minds of many graft is an accepted corollary of politics, the bulk of our members are financially honest. Those who aren't wear a brand as visible as the Mark of Zorro. Bribes as such are rare. We customarily consider 1200 bills during a session. A lobbyist who ladled out coin of the realm might soon empty his company's coffers. The principal suspicion of *quid pro quo* arises when a member puts in a bill that has a high nuisance effect on a particular industry. It may require all trains to creep at five miles an hour going through townships. It may impose unduly harsh penalties for selling beer to minors. If the sponsor has never before been interested in such matters, whispers are heard that he may be willing to kill his own bill—for the proper inducement.

Yet such episodes are isolated, especially in a legislature where most of the members come from farms and small towns. A politician from the metropolis can be known as a grafter and still survive. To begin with, he is more remote from his constituents. In addition, they are less likely to be troubled by the charge. Repeated police department shake-ups probably have inured them to this issue. But in the rural countryside, a legislator must be honest. He can get away with being

too liberal or too reactionary, but mutterings of corruption are more than he can weather.

Yet if the Senators and Representatives from the wide
open spaces are comparatively immune to propositions,
it is they who make the heaviest demands on the lobbyists for entertainment.

Many of them frankly have come to the legislature
for a good time. 'It's my biennial vacation,' a veteran
Senator from the sagebrush said to me. These men and
their wives or lady friends set a fast pace. They expect
steak dinners at the local hotel or American Legion
Club every night. They grumble over the lack of a
floor show. They ask for champagne. It was such grum-
bling that induced a worried lobbyist, with a crucial
bill on the docket the next day, to offer a statuesque
waitress $100 to scamper *au naturel* as part of the enter-
tainment.

'That wasn't bribery—except to the waitress,' he explained. 'It was merely sound public relations.'

Subservience to interests and lobbies in a legislature
does not necessarily involve currency changing hands
behind a convenient pillar or cloakroom door. As a
British versifier once remarked of his country's press:

> *You cannot hope to bribe or twist,*
> *Thank God, the British journalist;*
> *But seeing what the man will do*
> *Unbribed, there's no occasion to.*

Practically every one of us has his eye on a more
heavily braided political epaulet. Campaign funds are
important to this goal. It took a treasury of $65,000 to
elect one of our former colleagues to the governorship.
A state legislator who has favored keeping ax and saw

away from timberlands reserved for school revenues is hardly likely to have his gubernatorial dream financed by the big sawmill proprietors.

Today a new political factor has intruded. Since 1940 the population of Oregon has gone up 42 per cent. The state was predominantly rural a decade ago; now most of the people live inside city limits, and thousands of them belong to trade unions. No longer are the lobbyists for power and lumber, with their overflowing treasuries, the only ones to call the tune. Union representatives sit in the galleries and write down names as the roll calls proceed.

After a vote on industrial accident benefits, the square jawed CIO secretary said to a man who had sat in the Senate for a good number of years: 'I believe you'll regret your *nay* on that, my friend.'

The remark was passed without malice, but when I came back from lunch the Senator was still slumped in his chair, his face the color of the linen handkerchief that protruded from his pocket. Perhaps he was totting up the number of CIO loggers and longshoremen in his district. Yet labor has had far less influence in our legislature than management, possibly because management can finance so much more lavishly a bid for higher elective office.

The legislature generates its own social life, its rivalries for pre-eminence in the receiving line, and its own intrigues. Two downtown hotels in the capital house most of the members, although a few save money by doing their own cooking at motor courts. Barely a week of the session has gone by before the gossip is in full swing.

On the whole the legislators' conduct is decorous.

These men work hard—as they must to possess even a fragmentary knowledge of the bills being considered. Our state, for example, has an obscure statute exempting from the corporate income tax all businesses deriving 95 per cent of their receipts from property rentals, a strike of truly Klondike proportions for the real estate trade. Someone didn't catch that joker.

A distinguished member of the U. S. Senate once said to me: 'You get a little better perspective on things 3000 miles from home. The voters aren't looking right down your throat all the time. And it's a little more difficult for a handful of people to make it look like they represented the whole universe.'

I now know exactly what he meant. Recently I put my name to a bill which would limit the number of the billboards that make garish corridors out of our highways. A few men were naturally stung on what Justice Brandeis once called 'the pocket nerve.' They were soon able to make it seem as if the entire state was up in arms against the proposed law.

Although I had a perfect voting record on the A.F. of L. score-sheet, the head of the Signpainters' Union called me an 'enemy of labor,' and claimed that I wanted to throw hundreds of men out of work. Then the 'widows and orphans' began to appear: forlorn families which would become public charges if they no longer could rent their roadside property to the signboard companies. The state advertising club sent an impressive delegation, which accused me of being a foe of the Bill of Rights: The advertising men would lose their 'freedom of speech' if their billboards were barred from the countryside.

Although the bill had been suggested to me by a

wealthy old woman who loved the outdoors and did not like to see it defaced, my proposal was denounced by these delegations as being of Communist origin. Presently several Senators came to me and revoked their pledges to vote for the measure.

Put to a public referendum, I imagine the bill would have passed by at least 5 to 1. These few small pressure groups were able to induce the legislature to reject it overwhelmingly. I still marvel at the fact that the billboard owners themselves never once appeared during the entire operation. One can admire an enemy's technique, even while being victimized by it.

The head of the union later came to my desk somewhat shamefacedly. This lean Scotsman with the burr in his voice indicated that he didn't believe all the propaganda of the signboard people. He went along but he was not happy about it. 'I've told them,' he admitted, 'that they ought to stop plastering their boards in front of the scenery.'

III

The legislature has been compared to Congress, but it is only a pale shadow of the national lawmaking body.

Congress is in session at least six months and recently almost continually. It has a vast permanent staff. Nearly all of the members of Congress are in Washington, D. C., a far greater part of the year than in their home constituencies. Congress is an accepted fact of life. It is inevitable.

The state legislature is different. In all except ten states, it assembles only every other year. The staff rarely operates between meetings. The legislature frequently must start from scratch to recruit its clerks, stenographers, messengers, sergeants-at-arms, and innumerable other functionaries. Competition for the jobs is keen, and the two parties claw at each other over patronage. Because salaries are low, most of the posts go to residents of the capital city. The pay will not sustain someone who has to rent a hotel room, especially when rates are raised for the coming of the legislature and its huge retinue.

In spite of this largesse, the capital generally hates the legislature. The county that is the seat of state government in Oregon cast a heavy vote at referendum against raising legislative pay to $600 a year, although the proposal carried decisively in the state at large.

This has been uniformly true of attempts to increase legislators' salaries in numerous states. Residents of the capital justify their stand on the theory that they come into intimate contact with members of the legislature and realize their low caliber. I doubt if this is the real reason. I know the city officials and county commissioners who operate the community that is our state capital. They are no more capable than the members of the legislature. Although the state capital is one of the most picturesque communities in Oregon, the main line of a transcontinental railway is allowed to thread along the street that goes past the State Supreme Court Building. When a fast freight rumbles through, the temple of justice quivers and the justices must halt their deliberations.

State government is a law unto itself. The huge Federal bureaucracy is policed by Congress, and Congress sits most of the year. The legislature is the solitary brake on state government, and it operates only four months out of every twenty-four. Our state has 128 boards and commissions which are practically autonomous. The inhabitants of the capital work for these agencies. They frequently fear the legislature, for the legislature constitutes the sole threat to the little principalities they have created for themselves.

Our state government has no comptroller-general to patrol expenditures, no independent auditors to follow the taxpayer's dollar down to the last penny. I poked into an obscure bureau, which, unknown to the public, was paying its executive secretary $2000 more a year than the salary received by the Governor. This would have been impossible vis-à-vis the President under the rigid methods of supervision practiced in the Federal government. It would not have been dared, for fear of investigation by Congress.

Our legislature has deliberately been kept weak and irresponsible. Although we must approve the expenditure every biennium of nearly $1,000,000,000 wrested from the wallets and bank accounts of Oregon's people, our committees have lacked the authority to take testimony under oath! This testimony is not even taken down, yet on its presumable authenticity we levy taxes, fix penal sentences, and set educational standards. Although we of the State Senate must confirm appointments by the Governor, we never conduct a separate investigation but merely accept meekly his appraisal of his own appointees. If we examine critically the expenditures of a state agency, some newspaper can be depended upon to publish an editorial asking caustically why we don't adjourn and go home.

In common with twenty-three other states, we do not have a Legislative Reference Bureau. We must accept hearsay from lobbyists and state officials as to the facts

regarding bills which 1,620,000 people must obey or go
to jail. At one session we enacted a measure that doubled
the license fee on a 3000-pound private passenger car,
and yet at the same time actually reduced public utility
fees on some of the heaviest trucks and trailers weighing
more than 34,000 pounds. This may have been a 'sleeper'
but I am not sure. The bill was forty-three pages in
length and we had no analysis before us when the roll
call was taken. I voted *No* only because I did not know
the contents of the bill.

Taxes are becoming a grim burden in the United
States. Levies sit astride our shoulders as the Old Man
of the Sea weighed down Sinbad the Sailor. State taxes
are certainly a part of this load. State bureaucracy is no
different from Federal bureaucracy. It is self-perpetuat-
ing. Hundreds of its executives are empire builders.
Many of its niches are resting places for moribund politicians. Only the legislature can make sure that the citizen gets a dollar's value for a dollar spent. I am convinced
this never will happen in our states until each legislature has an arm equivalent to the General Accounting
Office at the Federal level.

To quote from the *Congressional Directory:* 'The
General Accounting Office is the agency of Congress designed to check on the financial transactions of the government.' Few state legislatures possess such binoculars.
In many of the forty-eight states, the government at the
state capital audits itself. Inefficiencies are examined by
the people responsible for them. The legislature does
not put officials on the witness stand and make them tell
in the presence of the Bible what has been occurring in
their departments.

Legislative debate should be taken down and printed. Only seven states, Connecticut, Maine, New York, North Dakota, Pennsylvania, Tennessee, and West Virginia record or reduce to shorthand the words spoken in the House and Senate. Maine and Pennsylvania alone among the forty-eight sovereignties publish the words of their lawmakers. This might make for more responsibility. It would discourage inaccuracies. Most state constitutions, in common with that of the United States, provide for legislative immunity to suits for libel or slander. This is an incitement to reckless utterance. When combined with the fact that legislative speeches are spoken into thin air and not recorded, the result often is bawdy-house language and the most blatant sort of falsehoods.

'The Federal system,' pointed out Adlai Stevenson, when he was Governor of Illinois, 'is the answer to the dangers of overcentralization in the United States. With forty-eight enlightened, progressive state capitals, there is little danger of too great consolidation of governmental authority.'

It is easy to forget the state capital in an era when the national government is building the hydrogen bomb and drafting eighteen-year-old's. New York collects what amounts to $61 from each of its men, women, and children every year. The state of Washington calls for $95 *per capita* and Oregon requests $72. Connecticut demands $54, and the state government at Sacramento must assess every resident of California $90 annually.

These are not trivial sums, when we remember that they are exacted from everyone between the bassinet and the cemetery. The seat of state government is very much a part of our lives and budgets. We will do well in the troubled days ahead to keep a watchful eye on the capital within our own particular states as well as on that more distant citadel of authority at Washington, D. C.

– 8 –

THE DAY WE PASSED

THE OATH BILL

I

THE day we passed the teacher's oath bill in the Oregon Senate was the most uncomfortable day I ever have spent during my service in minor political posts, which includes membership as an Oregon State Representative before the war and now as a State Senator.

It was unlike any other issue. An atmosphere of tension prevailed from the start. Ordinarily, the senators gossiped and bantered with each other before a day's session, trading opinions about the bills on the calendar for that particular date.

But on this day there was no swapping of early-morning views. A strange and ominous silence hung over most of us. A member of a veterans' organization to which I belong had come to my desk and said he hoped I would 'vote for America.' I told my veteran friend that according to the best of my poor lights I always voted for America. Aside from this, no one mentioned Senate

Bill 323. Curiously, however, I did overhear some minor observations about trivial bills on the docket.

A grim nervousness troubled me. It was a feeling I never had experienced when we debated a sales tax, or highway standards, or old-age assistance, or any other public question. But on what other question before a state legislature might your vote result in doubts about your patriotism? I even had sent to Portland for a copy of a letter of commendation from my wartime commanding officer, General O'Connor. I looked it over and the phrases reassured me: '. . . a person of integrity, loyalty and ability . . . faithful and diligent . . .'

I thought of the General standing in the clawing Arctic cold at Whitehorse and Big Delta, with the temperature at 66° below zero, exhorting his troops to build the wilderness highway and clear the tundra airfields. The General's muskrat-skin cap, I remembered, was always at a jaunty angle, no matter what the difficulties. Surely approval from such a man—West Point, '07—would stand me in good stead that day if my vote aroused the kind of unfounded suspicions we had been led to expect.

Perhaps some of our anxiety stemmed from the fact that we were so unprepared to endure the kind of political pressure endemic to this issue. There we sat on the Senate floor, in front of God and everybody. We did not even have offices to which we could go for sanctuary and meditation. All our whispered pre-session discussions were as public as a football game. On top of all this, we virtually were serving without pay. Yet we were expected to stand up to a question as full of bitterness and hostility as any before the national Congress.

Several of my colleagues had tried hard to bottle up the bill in committee. They were opposed to a teacher's

oath, felt it was bad legislation. Yet, now that the measure had been forced to the floor, I knew they intended
to cast a *Yea* vote. They had brilliant careers ahead of
them in the Republican party. They could not afford to
have their patriotism and loyalty impugned.

There was some advantage, I reflected sadly, to being
in the minority party in a one-party state. At least, you
probably weren't going anywhere. You could vote your
own convictions without fearing you had cost yourself
the governorship and political glory.

The first speeches for the bill were reasonably calm
and logical. Why should anyone hesitate to sign such an
oath in a period of national crisis? But, then, the speeches
began to take on fire and brimstone. Hearst editorials
were quoted, and so were statements by U. S. Senator
McCarthy. Some of the most zealous promoters of
loyalty oaths for schoolteachers turned out to be Senators who had sponsored bills calling for greater financial
returns to the operators of pari-mutuel racetracks, to
promoters of irrigation districts and to fly-by-night stock
salesmen.

As I mused on the irony of this, a Republican Senator strolled over and sat beside me at my walnut desk.
'How are you going to vote?' he asked.

'I believe against the bill,' I said somewhat tenta-
tively.

'Then I will, too,' he said and returned to his own
chair.

This had never happened before. On many measures
a Senator often was willing to cast a solitary *Nay* vote.
Indeed, it could be a sign of independence. But this was
not the case on the oath bill. No one desired to be without partners on such an issue. In fact, the brief visit

from my Republican colleague helped considerably to
fortify my own attitude. Truth compels me to admit
that I still am uncertain how I would have voted had I
been completely alone in opposition to the bill. His visit
bolstered my courage.

As the speeches went on it was evident that only a
comparatively few members of the Senate felt strongly
on the issue. They were making all the noise. The great
majority sat in silence. In my opinion, they were ill at
ease. A demagogic speech, with much flag-waving, was
made by a so-called New Deal Democrat. It provoked
some embarrassed glances, but no applause. I knew he
had been elected to the Senate with endorsements from
both the A.F. of L. and CIO. I looked up at the gallery
where sat the gray-haired retired teacher who represented the Teachers Union at the legislature. Her usually serene face was drawn and taut. Some of labor's
chickens were coming home to roost.

Finally, the first talk was made against the bill. A
youthful radio station manager who served on the
Senate Education Committee wanted to know why
teachers had been singled out. Bob Holmes asked for
specific evidence of disloyalty among Oregon schoolteachers. I may have been mistaken, but I thought his
speech stirred some admiration on the floor.

My own remarks were relatively short. I called to the
attention of my fellow Democrats the fact that President
Truman had vetoed the McCarran Bill. I reminded the
Republicans that their most popular public figure,
Dwight D. Eisenhower, had taken a positive position
against teacher oaths when he was president of Columbia University. I pointed out that only a few days earlier the Senate had set the oath to be taken by circuit

judges *pro tem*. It was the standard oath of allegiance
to the state and national constitutions—no test oath at
all. In other words, the Senate was alarmed about the
loyalty of schoolteachers but evidently not about that of
a man who would wield life-and-death powers on the
bench. Was Earl Warren unpatriotic? As Governor of
California, he had opposed the faculty oath at the State
University. I closed with a quotation from Paul G.
Hoffman which warned against the hysteria of witch-
hunting.

The speeches resumed and at last we voted. The bill
passed 25 to 5.

II

Of 12 members of the Oregon Senate who were originally elected with the endorsement of organized labor,
only three voted against the oath bill. In view of the
fact that the national policy of both the CIO and the
A.F. of L. is emphatically against this type of legislation, the record would seem to confirm a recent claim
in Portland by U. S. Senator Wayne L. Morse to the
effect that trade unions have not been sufficiently 'selec-
tive and discriminating' about whom they back for public office. Furthermore, at least three of labor's endorsees
delivered vehement speeches for the bill. Indeed, they
were the main orators on the issue!

The five who voted *Nay* were a diverse lot. Three
were Democrats, two Republicans. One was a Union
Pacific railroad brakeman, a Mormon, from the rugged
Blue Mountains of Oregon. Another was the manager
of radio station KAST. A third was a wealthy logging-
equipment wholesaler who drove a big tan Cadillac and
was lay head of the Presbyterian Church synod in the

state. Another was a quiet, earthy farmer who was a bell-
wether of the most conservative wing of the G.O.P., although he told me after the vote that he was pleased to
learn that Mr. Eisenhower opposed teacher oaths. And
there was I, a journalist.

After we had adjourned for the day, a group of war
veterans clustered at the rear of the chamber. They
asked the reason for my vote. I reminded them that the
lobbyists for some of the veterans organizations had
spent many hours trying to lobby through the oath bill.
Then I showed these veterans a bill from the U. S. Veterans' Administration, a model act in force in most of
the states. This bill proposed to limit the fee that a
bank or lawyer could assess for administering the estate
of a veteran who was in a mental institution. While the
lobbyists for the veterans' groups had been spending
their time on teachers' oaths, the banks had destroyed
the effectiveness of the model bill to safeguard the
finances of veterans who had lost their sanity. I had protested as a member of the Military Affairs Committee
but received no backing. The protest had failed. I said
to the assembled veterans in the Senate chamber:

'I may be wrong, but I should think that spokesmen
for veterans' organizations ought to be more concerned
about the welfare of men who have been mentally dam-
aged fighting on the field of battle for the United States
than in foisting special oaths on schoolteachers.'

The veterans stayed on a long time. The heat and
anger were gone. No further resentment was voiced.
The contrast of the two bills had made an impression.
I felt sure that the rank and file of these war veterans
had no real personal interest in the question of a teacher's oath.

Lunch that day in the Senate lounge was a dismal occasion. One or two of the speakers for the oath bill ate their sandwiches with gusto and talked of the victory. But most of the Senators munched and said little. As I looked around me in the lounge, I could see that the so-called normal measurements of liberalism and conservatism were no gauge in such a fight. The oath bill had been supported by men who regularly voiced the aphorisms of the New Deal, who always voted against the corporations and with the 'common people.' On the other hand, one of the adversaries of the oath bill was a Hoover Republican who made a fetish of governmental economy and who talked frequently for 'the old-fashioned virtues.'

Suddenly I realized that there was a whole lot to the old-fashioned virtues, after all—particularly when a citizen believed in them with sufficient faith to brave political perils in their defense. All at once, integrity seemed more important to me than ideology. As one of the youngest members of the Senate, I fear that this was a comparatively new set of values. In the past, zeal had dictated otherwise.

One of the conservatives said to me, 'I am glad you and I voted together against the oath bill. It shows that freedom is more important than the budget.' Perhaps he knew what I had been thinking, for his words paraphrased my thoughts.

It was not an historic or world-shaking episode and it occurred in a state with 1 per cent of the national population. Yet it told me many things. Liberalism may have more to do with the heart than with the stomach. And we do not tread the trail of Jefferson just because we may remark occasionally that Jefferson was a great man.

Did not the President buried at Monticello tell us that 'each generation must make its own fight for liberty'?

Looking back, I have decided that the day we passed Senate Bill 323 was one brief sortie in that fight. But there was no clear division as to sides, and this will make me more circumspect in my political judgments during the future.

Yet I must add the auspicious footnote that the teacher's oath never became law. Our brief fight, however futile in terms of Senate votes, alerted many forces in the state. This included not only schoolteachers but also the faculties of the University and State College, who saw that they would be next. The woman lobbying for the Teachers' Union helped to enlist the intervention of two influential editors, Charles Sprague of the *Salem Statesman* and William M. Tugman of the *Eugene Register-Guard*.

But not even this combination could have beaten the bill, had it reached the floor. Political fright and ambition would have prevailed over reason. The liberals triumphed by a stratagem frequently used by the reactionaries. They kept the bill locked in committee until the clock ran out at adjournment time.

'I don't necessarily approve of the tactic of denying a vote on the floor,' Maurine later told a group of Parent-Teacher leaders. 'Yet,' she continued, 'I believe many members of the House were grateful for it. They did not like the teacher's oath bill, but they were afraid to vote against it. By holding the bill in committee, we saved their consciences and also saved the state.'

This tenuous victory may yet prove to be permanent. The American Legion soon had a new state commander, Karl Wagner, who said that no Oregon schoolteachers had been shown to be Communistic and subversive, and that the Legion would not humiliate loyal teachers by forcing an oath upon them. He said that the standard oath to support the Constitutions of the state and nation had proved sufficient.

And so Oregon today, for all its conservatism, is one of the few states in the country without special test oath legislation. Never again will I regard a lost fight in the Senate as valueless. Had we sat silent when the oath bill passed our arm of the Legislature 25 to 5, it probably would have been law long before this.

– 9 –

FROM THE SOD TO THE

SIDEWALK

I

WHEN political scientists discuss state government, one theme threads through their proceedings. What about the rural domination of legislatures? A legend surrounds this. It is that farm people themselves demand such supremacy. They would rebel without it. Maurine and I believed the legend, until we learned otherwise.

One of our colleagues constantly told us that he, personally, favored setting up new districts to give cities and towns additional representation. 'But,' he interpolated, 'the rural voters in my county would tear me limb from limb, they would saw me in half lengthwise, I would disappear from political ken. I have to oppose reapportionment to save my hide.'

We believed him and sympathized with him. After all, we did not expect our colleague to take his life in his hands to support reapportionment, which is a fancy term for the process involved in shaping legislative districts to conform to changing population patterns.

After many years of being stalled and delayed by the legislature, trade unions and the League of Women Voters circulated petitions to place the issue of reapportionment on the ballot. In the rural constituency of our colleague the vote was 8005 against reapportionment and 17,322 for reapportionment.

Abruptly, we realized that our colleague had been voicing his own fears and prejudices rather than those of the farmers in his district. The farmers saw the problem as citizens. He saw it exclusively as a politician, in the framework of what he interpreted to be his own self-interest.

Ever since this episode, we have wondered how many legislative rotten boroughs exist in America because politicians insist upon making out their farm constituents to be as selfish and grasping as they are—when this is emphatically not the case.

And yet these rotten boroughs help to distort the whole process of state lawmaking, to prevent it from living up to the needs of the atomic age and the twentieth century.

II

In ancient times the voice of the sovereign was infinitely more powerful than that of anyone else. The Magna Charta and much later the American Revolution helped end this tyranny.

Yet today, well on toward two centuries after the troops of George III surrendered at Yorktown, the United States contains hundreds of lopsided rotten boroughs where the vote of one man may possess 350 times the strength of that of his neighbor in another district. Can free institutions survive under such conditions?

The city dwellers of this country are denied their fair share of seats in state capitols, where our laws are made. This denial exists in spite of the fact that it violates the Federal Constitution and the constitutions of many of the individual states.

The 4,125,000 urban residents of Los Angeles County have one Senator in the California legislature. Equal Senate representation with them is enjoyed by the 13,560 rural inhabitants of Mono and Inyo Counties. What rare quality, perhaps peculiar to the remote Sierra Nevada Range, renders an Inyo County sheep rancher worthy of at least 300 times the strength in the California Senate of a Los Angeles surgeon or trolley conductor?

The hard and simple fact is that America has moved to town but its state legislatures have not. In spite of the lure of green fields, the migration from sod to pavement continues. Never has the trend been so persistent as during the past ten years. Millions of city dwellers once lived in the countryside. In a period of unprecedented agricultural prosperity the proportion of Americans carried on the census rolls as 'rural farm' has steadily declined until today it is at its lowest ebb in the nation's history. The Bureau of the Census has announced that only 23,577,000 people still make their homes on farms. This figure is a mere 16 per cent of the total population. The Department of Agriculture has expressed alarm at the decrease of 6,000,000 farm workers in the last four years as a threat to food production.

This significant migration has taken place in face of the fact that the farm has never seemed so appealing, particularly from afar. In spite of the vacillating program of the Eisenhower administration with respect to agriculture, farm debt has never been so low, perhaps because of previous prosperity. In addition, giant transmission systems have brought electricity to farms and ranches in even the most remote valleys. In 1933 only 27 per cent of Oregon's farms had electricity. Today the figure is 98 per cent. Never before has the typical farm family enjoyed so many of the creature comforts of modern life. Why, then, are Americans leaving the farm in such numbers?

In a Portland drug store, a rangy, talkative lad with sideburns explained why he had moved to the city. 'Living with my folks at the apple orchard was all right,' he said, 'but I didn't see fellows or girls from one week to the next. When I went to the city waiting to be drafted, I could see other young folks nearly all the time. After I got out of the Army I headed for the city again. It's where I have a better time.' This citizen of twenty-two is speaking not for himself alone. He is voicing the feelings of millions of other gregarious Americans who have pilgrimaged to cities during the past decade.

And yet, in spite of the unceasing migration to the cities, a comparatively small force of rural America is raising vastly more crops today than ever before. Mechanization alone has made this possible. A single farm hand can cultivate as many acres as six or seven did a few years ago. Without this mechanization the hegira from farm to city would have brought about a genuine crisis in the nation's food production. As it is, some farms are pressed for robust help because most of the men and women moving to the cities have been from 20 to 35 years of age. It is significant that 25 per cent of urban dwellers now fit into this age category as compared with only 18 per cent of farm residents.

At Washington State College, an agricultural school, a cross-section of co-eds was sampled on marriage preferences. Doctors, lawyers, journalists, and businessmen all were rated by many of these women, themselves from farms, as more desirable husbands than farmers. These were typical reasons:

'Farm life is lonely and remote.'

'Schools and recreation for children are inferior.'

'I am too accustomed to friends to enjoy solitude and isolation.'

Many responsible farm leaders believe rural life must be made more attractive to young men and women. The Oregon State Grange is sponsoring various social events to help hold the next generation on the farm. In Montana the Farmers' Union has suggested frequent get-togethers to overcome backwoods loneliness. Projects have been encouraged such as amateur theatricals, pot-luck suppers, modern dance groups for farm girls, and bookmobiles to take the latest best-sellers from farm to farm. 'We have worked hard to get electric power lines to every single rural home,' explains Elmer McClure, Master of the Oregon State Grange. 'We realize that comforts and convenience are essential if the farm is to succeed in competition with the obvious lure of the city.'

After V-J Day, in August of 1945, the teeming cities of the Pacific Coast braced themselves for a great exodus. Thousands of newcomers had migrated from farms on the Great Plains or in the Inter-mountain region. Chambers of Commerce freely predicted that these people would return to the land now that the war was

over. Many did—for a time. Then they started coming
back into town.

An industrial depression is one of the few develop-
ments which might make former rural residents go back
to the soil. Between 1930 and 1935, for example, the
national impetus toward pavement and factories was reversed. Rural population actually increased during this
period in proportion to the country's total. But as long
as full employment continues, the ever-burgeoning metropolis probably will make further inroads on the dwin-
dling percentage of Americans who make their homes
on farms.

III

Legislatures are usually the sole judge of their membership. In other words, legislatures must reapportion
themselves if the expanding urban population is to receive the seats its numbers merit under the Jeffersonian
idea of 'one man, one vote.' This means that many rural
Senators and Representatives must be willing to abol-
ish their own niches. In politics, never a realm particularly distinguished for altruism, this just is not done.
Rural politicians are in the saddle and they do not intend to dismount voluntarily.

I use the term 'rural politicians' advisedly. They
should be sharply distinguished from rural people as a
whole. I am convinced that the average farmer does not
want any more representation in the legislature than is
his just share. I realize this statement may be challenged
by people struggling for fair legislative apportionment
in many states, but in Oregon we have proof to sustain
the claim.

Young Democrats and Young Republicans joined to-

gether to place on the ballot a referendum requiring
the legislature to be districted according to population, as
the state constitution stipulates. The League of Women
Voters and the A.F. of L. and the CIO participated in
the effort. This was thought to end the list of sponsoring organizations. But the Grange, the largest farm organization in the state, approved the measure, too.

'Farmers are not going to act like the dog-in-the-man-
ger,' said Elmer McClure, Master of the Oregon State
Grange.

The reapportionment bill was enacted at the polls by
the decisive margin of 357,550 votes to 194,292. Still
more significant, it carried in nearly every rural county,
including the areas of largest agricultural income. Rural
people had shown that the rural politicians did not
speak for them, when it came to denying city folks equity
in the legislature.

I am convinced that rural politicians thwarting reapportionment often are confederates of some of the
most reactionary elements in their states. Vest-pocket
constituencies are made to order for groups blocking social progress. The Grange made a study of legislative
roll calls and found far more backing for public education in rural areas from urban Senators and Representatives than from men who spoke for rotten boroughs in
the backwoods.

In its study, the State Grange discovered that legislators from backwoods rotten boroughs often served not
their own constituents but great financial interests se-
questered in the very cities these rural legislators pre-
tended to find so repugnant. The farmers and ranchers
got the oratory, the banks and utility corporations got
the roll-call votes.

Although I have been bitterly criticized in Oregon politics as a symbol of the big city, namely Portland, it is not without considerable significance that the State Grange gave me the highest rating of any of the thirty members of the Senate, on its so-called 'score card.'

I was recorded as having eleven 'favorable' votes and one 'unfavorable' vote on roll calls that the Grange considered crucial to agriculture. The one adverse vote, incidentally, was in favor of legalizing the sale of colored margarine! But on issues where rural families were pitted against groups that wanted to grab natural resources or choke off rural electrification, I received a higher rank from the Grange than did many Senators who claimed to speak for farming areas.

Grange Master McClure said to me, 'We have learned that a man's place of residence has little to do with his political sympathies. We have learned it is possible for a man to come from the sidewalks of Portland and still be a champion of the family-sized farm operator. Your wife helped to get through a program for educating retarded children, when the place which probably needed the program the least was Portland, because it already had made a start in that direction. I think a whole lot of our farm people are going to think twice before they ever conclude again that a legislator is automatically against them because he lives in the city and automatically for them because he lives in the country. Far more depends upon the legislator himself than upon where he hangs his hat!'

When we tried to repeal the loophole in the state corporation tax law which exempted profitable multi-million-dollar office buildings in Portland, the effort failed because many of the loudest Portland-hating legislators came to the rescue of Portland's biggest real-estate monopolies.

Yet, at last, the issue of a fair apportionment of legislative seats reached the ballot, and the combination of big-city corporations and backwoods lawmakers was effectively rebuked. Although the Oregon legislature had consistently rejected bills for new districts in the House and Senate, the people approved the idea overwhelmingly.

But in states without the initiative and referendum, or where these instruments of democracy have never been used in behalf of reapportionment, some weird travesties on representative government have resulted.

Hartford and Colebrook each has two members in the Connecticut House of Representatives. The population of Hartford is 166,000, that of Colebrook 547. Los Angeles and San Francisco together contain practically 50 per cent of California's residents, but qualify for only 5 per cent of the Senate desks at Sacramento. Baltimore has 48 per cent of Maryland's people, yet only 29 per cent of the state's legislators. The Minnesota constitution, like that of Oregon, requires legislative zones of substantially the same population. Yet some House districts have 7500 people, others 65,000. Silver Bow County, where Butte's copper miners live, has 47,990 inhabitants and one Montana State Senator. Mineral County, with 2062 people, similarly has one Senator.

The Colorado House of Representatives is supposed to be just what its name implies—a forum where the residents of a great mountain state receive fair representation. But although the districts are presumed to be of equal population, Washington County has one House member for 7550 people while Jefferson County has one

House member for seven times this many people: 55,687.

Approximately half of America's total automobile mileage is traveled inside city limits. Yet the legislatures of the country have allotted only a pitiful 10 per cent of gasoline tax revenues to the upkeep of city streets.

Richard L. Maher of the *Cleveland Press* has pointed out that although the bulk of Ohio's cigaret tax money is collected in the metropolitan regions the 'cornstalk brigade' in the legislature has seen to it that 'not one urban school district can qualify for these funds, although some were on the verge of closing their schools.'

Paradoxically, these inequities tend to compound themselves because the forty-eight state legislatures have the power to set the boundaries of the country's Congressional districts. This means that the rural dominance in state capitals is inevitably transplanted to Capitol Hill in Washington, D. C. Senator Paul H. Douglas of Illinois has written in *The New York Times:* 'Rural-dominated State Legislatures have frequently refused to reapportion Congressional districts in accordance with changes in population. As a result, opinions of city dwellers are minimized and opinions of those who live in the country and small towns are maximized.'

The national House of Representatives has 435 members. Under the U. S. Constitution the districts must be based on population. This means each Congressman should have approximately the same number of constituents. Yet the lofty constitutional mandate, handed down to us by the founders of the Republic, is honored only in the breach.

In my own state the Portland Congressional district contains 471,537 men, women, and children. The 2nd district, a domain of vast grain and cattle ranches, has barely half this many residents—247,383. Similar examples can be cited from all over the nation. In Seattle it takes 527,768 people to qualify for a member in the House of Representatives. But in the 3rd Washington district, only 321,162 people are represented by a Congressman. Yet the national Constitution dictates that these districts should be of equal population!

There is hardly a state where the Constitution is not similarly thwarted. In Texas the 8th district has a population of 806,000, while the 17th district contains only 226,000. And always it is the city which gets stuck. The 17th district is rural but the under-represented 8th district is the metropolitan area centering around Houston.

Representative Samuel W. Yorty (D. Calif.), for example, speaks for 480,827 constituents in the state's 26th District, while Representative Donald L. Jackson (R. Calif.), the man who impugned the patriotism of Methodist Bishop Bromley Oxnam, speaks for 223,703 in the same state's 16th District.

Be the states vast like California or of postage-stamp dimensions like Connecticut, legislatures invariably seem to have trouble with their arithmetic. Thus Representative Thomas J. Dodd (D. Conn.) has 539,661 constituents in the state's 1st District while Representative James T. Patterson (R. Conn.), in the same state's 5th District, has a mere 274,300 constituents. And these are not obscure numbers. They mean that each resident of the under-populated district has twice the voice in the House as each resident of the over-populated district.

The difference within states are no sharper than the discrepancies between different states. The ratio of almost 4 to 1 between the number of constituents represented by certain House members is actually greater than the contrast in the constituencies represented by the U. S. Senators from Michigan and Kansas, respectively. Yet our form of government has relied on a Senate apportioned geographically and a House meticulously divided as to population. Obviously, mathematics have gone awry when one Ohio district in the House has 545,000 residents and another Ohio district materially less than half this number of people—227,000.

Lopsided legislatures are rarely inclined to organize nicely balanced Congressional districts. The urge to self-preservation among politicians shames that among the beasts of jungle and tundra. Most unbalanced legislatures craftily carve up the map to serve the personal political ambitions of State Senators and State Representatives who yearn to answer roll calls in the national Congress.

The result has been neglect of urban problems in the one branch of Congress where city and town dwellers, because of their preponderant numbers, might expect to have their welfare zealously promoted. Such issues as housing, race relations, traffic jams, school lunches, and public assistance are often peculiar to metropolitan areas. But the House of Representatives has ceased to be a forum where these questions are preoccupying.

The national House is reapportioned every ten years, when a census is taken. Some states lose seats, other states gain. This is when the state legislatures are turned loose with a cleaver, to chop states into new Congressional districts, and almost invariably, city folks suffer.

Because Missouri has lost two Congressmen, its legislature has drawn up new zones which require St. Louis districts to have 450,000 people apiece while some rural districts need have only 317,000 people. The *St. Louis*

Post-Dispatch has complained that urban voters will be left 'with cut-rate ballots, which lose value as the population grows.'

Representative Emanuel Celler of New York, chairman of the House Judiciary Committee, has introduced a bill to put teeth into the long-dormant reapportionment provisions of the U. S. Constitution. The bill would require each Congressional district to be compact and contiguous, not more than 15 per cent off in population, when compared with the average of other districts in the state. Each district would have to contain somewhere between 300,000 and 400,000 residents. If the district did not conform to these standards, the Congressman from the district would be denied his seat in the House. This is the kind of punishment that a politician understands and respects.

Mr. Celler's bill has mustered impressive support. *The New York Times* has declared that some such drastic bludgeon may be necessary to cope with 'the reluctance of State Legislatures to alter the boundaries of Congressional districts in conformity with the growth in population.'

Yet the disdain of legislators for city folks is often expressed in wondrous ways. I sat in our Senate listening to the reasons why rural mail carriers should be exempt from payment of the state gasoline tax. As soon as the bill had passed overwhelmingly, I suggested that corresponding tax benefits be conferred by the state on city letter carriers, who were even more underpaid and had to pound their routes on foot.

My colleagues guffawed loudly. They had never heard of such a thing. Why, it just didn't make good sense!

A few days later Maurine and I had fried chicken and

country gravy at her mother's 120-acre dairy farm, along foaming Salmon Creek. The RFD man came with the mail just as we were taking our leave. He was indignant that the Senate had ridiculed my proposal to give relief to his letter-carrying brethren in the cities.

And so we were encouraged once more to know that a gap deep and wide exists between rural politicians and rural people.

– 10 –

IT COSTS TOO MUCH TO

RUN FOR OFFICE

I

In our brief and amateur foray into politics, my wife and I have encountered one evil which looms above all others. This is the political campaign fund.

The nation has many laws against bribes and bribery. We become sanctimonious over public officials caught accepting an unethical dollar. But where does bribery leave off and a campaign contribution begin?

If Maurine or I ever would take $100 in cash behind the locked door of a hotel room to cast our vote for or against a specific legislative bill, we would be guilty of receiving a bribe. If apprehended, we would go to jail in disgrace—as we should.

But if, at the next election, we accept not $100 in cash but $1000 in a check from the same donor, it is all perfectly legal, providing the check is made out to the Neuberger-for-election committee.

What kind of hypocrisy is this?

If a public official should not be obligated to private

parties, why is a bribe outside the law while a campaign donation of almost any proportion is completely proper? The debt presumably still exists. Specific *quid pro quo* may not have been mentioned. Yet, realities are inexorable. Why should the American people delude themselves about anything so serious and important to them as their own self-government?

If a member of the legislature takes a campaign contribution from the owner of a gambling syndicate, can that member cast a roll-call vote to outlaw slot machines? If a member of the legislature is helped financially in his campaign by stockholders in a utility company, is he free to favor public power plants on the rivers of the state? If a member of a legislature has had his campaign radio broadcasts paid for by the owners of packing houses, can he be his own master when a bill for strict meat inspection comes before the House or Senate?

These questions, in my opinion, answer themselves. Yet campaign contributions—big campaign contributions—are part of our political structure. We blithely take them for granted. They rarely become topics of discussion at election time. But is not the phrase 'free government' sadly inappropriate when a man or woman can enter high office indebted for thousands and even millions of dollars in donations from all sorts of sources?

In 1860 the Republican National Committee spent $100,000 to elect Abraham Lincoln. A Presidential campaign fund fifty or sixty times this size is no longer uncommon. In 1912 a physician named Harry Lane spent a grand total of $923 becoming a U. S. Senator from Oregon. The most recent campaign of a successful Senatorial aspirant in our Western state cost over $70,000.

And Senator Paul H. Douglas even has spoken of holding down campaign treasuries in the larger industrial
states to something like $375,000. Added Senator Doug-
las, facetiously, I hope: 'A candidate should be able to
"jog along" with such a sum as this.'

Yet Senator Douglas could have set his sights too low.
In 1950 the committees backing the re-election cam-
paign of the late Senator Robert A. Taft spent $511,000.
The Republican state organization, also supporting
Taft, disbursed $1,297,000. And the *St. Petersburg
Times* has estimated that the two major adversaries in
the Florida Democratic Senatorial primaries that same
year spent nearly $2,000,000 between them.

Just to send one mailed appeal to every registered
voter in our legislative districts would have cost Maurine
and me a minimum of $5000! Nor does this involve first-
class postage. It also presupposes a good deal of volun-
teer assistance in addressing and stuffing envelopes. Needless to add, the Neubergers did not reach all their constituents by mail.

In our little races for the relatively insignificant offices of State Senator and State Representative, Maurine
and I have been extremely 'choosy' about who contributed to our campaign funds. We have never accepted
funds from any person or place which implied support
of a cause we could not sincerely endorse. Yet this is a
luxury available to widely-known people seeking comparatively unimportant positions. What if we were running for great contested offices such as U. S. Senator or
Governor? Could we be so finicky about the origins of
our campaign finances? With the Republicans in Oregon backed generally by big timber, big utilities, big
contractors, and big liquor and beer, can Democrats ever

pay for a single TV show or brochure printing if they insist upon being entirely ethical about political donations? No sterner dilemma faces a prospective candidate.

I still remember vividly what happened back in 1948, when the suggestion originally was made by members of our minority party that I try to become Oregon's first Democratic U. S. Senator since 1914. Shortly after this glorious and tempting vista was unfolded, I bumped headlong into a stubborn obstacle:

How would my campaign be financed?

I was informed that an adequate Senatorial campaign throughout the vast State of Oregon, which is nearly twice the area of New York, would require an absolute minimum of $40,000. I had no more idea where to raise such an amount of money than I have of where Captain Kidd's treasure is buried. In fact, I made an effort to finance a campaign and I might just as well have spent the time searching for the lost loot of the buccaneer.

Oregon's dominant industry is lumbering and the timber companies, like most large companies, make substantial campaign contributions. As a member of the state legislature, however, I had sponsored a bill to regulate logging practices in the forests. All the big timber companies opposed my bill, so that source was closed. One by one I went down the list—utilities, banks, real estate firms, liquor concerns. Mainly I had opposed their legislative proposals. No campaign funds there for me.

A Democratic party wheel horse in Oregon mentioned a splurging operator of slot machines. I was told this man was 'rolling in dough' and might like to have a Senator grateful to him. I wondered about the *quid pro quo*. Nothing at all tangible, I was informed, except that the slot-machine operator might value 'a little friendly Senatorial advice' should he perhaps have trouble with some obstreperous Government agency. It seemed a modest request, yet were these the terms on which one ascends to an office as exalted as the United States Senate?

Two possible sources remained—my personal friends and the trade unions. I consulted my friends. None of them is rich, but at least a dozen were good for $100 each. One would put up $500. Yet I was uncomfortable. The money was not deductible from taxes. I knew that the young doctor promising $500 might drive his old car a year longer because of this generosity. I did not want $100 if it meant that a friend's wife would wait a few extra months for that new dress.

Then there were the labor organizations. The incumbent senior Senator voted for the Taft-Hartley bill and the unions hoped to beat him. But the CIO in Oregon had less than $900 in its political action treasury. A close personal friend in the A.F. of L. gave me the most hope. This man, James T. Marr of the State Federation of Labor, felt his organization 'might' be able to raise $5000. I wondered, too, what obligations I would carry on my shoulders if I went to the Senate almost exclusively on labor financing. I have been generally sympathetic to labor's views, but the stocking of a campaign treasury should come from more than one group.

I was told by a veteran United States Representative from the region, a man who had served many terms in office, that 'a fellow in politics who insists on being lily-white, especially when it comes to accepting campaign funds, soon may find he has left the gate wide open to those who are as black as the Hole of Calcutta.' Integrity is a cherished standard, even by those who honor it

in the breach. No one wants to feel that a 'For Sale' sign
is implanted in his conscience. When I came to add up
my definite pledges, the possibles, the tentative $5000
from the Democratic National Committee, it totaled
$18,900—a far cry indeed from the $70,000 the backers
of the senior Senator had spent getting him elected. Furthermore, the Republican State committee would have
at least twenty times as much as the Democratic organization backing me. This estimate of the disparity in
funds between the two parties was extremely conservative, I later discovered.

Now it used to be that a man with a few dollars, a
sturdy throat, and principles firmly held could stump a
sprawling state effectively. Oswald West, whom Lincoln
Steffens described as a 'spectacularly progressive' Governor of Oregon in 1910, still lives. I went to hear what
he had to say.

'I was elected with $3000,' the ex-Governor remi-
nisced. 'All the money came from my own bank account
and that of one friend. Today $3000 would just about
buy you half an hour on a state-wide radio hookup.
Folks once came from miles around by horse and buckboard to attend a political rally. Now they wait for you
to go into their homes by radio and newspaper advertising or direct mail. That takes a lot of money. It makes
a candidate reliant on outside financing, unless he happens to be a very rich man. His independence is reduced. He becomes committed to the labor unions or
the real estate interests or some other special group.'

The ex-Governor, nearing eighty, rubbed his lean
chin thoughtfully. 'I've been active in politics in our
state for half a century,' he said. 'Oregon now has nearly
three times as many people as when I was Governor. Yet

political rallies are far less fully attended. There are too many competing attractions. This elevates the power of money in politics. A big campaign treasury must be raised, because it is so much more expensive to get your message to the voters.'

Formerly the candidate and a few personal associates wrote his political tracts. Now advertising men take over. Press agents must be hired. Like a circus, a candidate touring the state is preceded by an advance agent with a generous expense account. An advertising firm active in sponsoring many Oregon Congressmen and Governors recently outlined for me a campaign budget.

To herald my excellence with lapel buttons, matchbook covers, and nail files alone would cost $10,000. A photographer's bill in one campaign in the nearby state of Washington came to more than $3000. The candidate had to be snapped drying dishes, gaffing a salmon, pitching hay, picking apples. It mattered not that ordinarily he did none of these things. It was a way to 'sell' him to the voters in a handsomely illustrated brochure.

The situation in Oregon and Washington is not unique; it is paralleled in forty-six other states and wherever an election is held. The simple fact that it costs too much to run for office keeps many able individuals out of public life.

II

A generation ago, during the prohibition era, the famous Wickersham Commission warned that 'in the main the funds which make successful political campaigns come from the owners and habitués of vice, gambling and bootlegging resorts.'

This has been happening again today, only on a far

more extravagant scale because all campaign costs have been boosted enormously by TV time selling at $31,000 per half hour.

Once the voters were reached by torchlight parades and boisterous rallies, as my friend Oswald West explained. These were comparatively inexpensive. A brass band and tossing banners would be the sole out-of-pocket items. Men and women would drive all day to listen to a speaker like Woodrow Wilson or Fighting Bob La Follette.

The Kefauver committee heard testimony that a huge sum had been contributed by the operator of pari-mutuel dog tracks in Florida to the campaign fund of Governor Fuller Warren, Florida being one of the few states which legalizes greyhound racing. Testimony was given before the committee that the head of a union of municipal employees had secretly passed $10,000 in cash to ex-Mayor O'Dwyer of New York on the veranda of Gracie Mansion as a political donation.

But the public learns about episodes of this kind only when Congressional committees, armed with Federal sleuths and the power of subpoena, can dig and search for months. Most of the time the voters never really know who pays for the billboards, the luxurious hotel headquarters, the pretty models who hand out buttons and literature.

One afternoon I sat in the office of a leading business-man in Portland. 'I suppose you saw in the papers where I was listed for a contribution of $3000,' said the businessman and he mentioned the campaign of a prominent candidate for Governor. 'Well,' he continued, 'I hate to admit this, but I never put up that sum at all. In a moment of weakness, I agreed to let them use my name to conceal some shady money they couldn't properly account for without suffering political damage. They had to name someone respectable as a contributor, and so they named me.'

As I left the businessman's office, I speculated on the probable source of the suspicious $3000. I decided it was the underworld—gamblers, procurers, and their ilk. But the people had been led to believe that the money came from a pillar of the community.

Oregon has one of the sternest corrupt-practices laws in the nation, an act drafted to control spending in political campaigns. If a blindfold could be slipped so easily over the voters' eyes in Oregon, I wondered about the many other states where no effective corrupt-practices laws exist at all.

The fact of the matter is that restraints on campaign slush funds ceased to function in the United States when the inflation of World War II began. Where nickels and dimes once would put a candidate into office, greenbacks suddenly became a prerequisite. Today, no holds are barred. Managers of political races frequently pick up money wherever they can get it. Upright and honest nominees are committed without consultation to back-hall deals by men who must keep the campaign coffers filled. After the votes have been counted, the victorious candidate may abruptly discover that he does not enter office as unfettered as he had imagined.

The Governor of an important state said to me, 'I personally reimbursed a man for a very substantial campaign contribution, when my managers told me that a large string was tied to it—the man wanted to say who should be the new Commandant of State Police.' Of course, not all candidates can afford to use their own funds to free themselves. Should honesty in office be the privilege mainly of the rich and well-born?

No hard and fast rule governs the motives behind political donations. I have seen an effort made to attach conditions to a $50-dollar contribution. On the other hand, some public-spirited man may give $1000 or more merely because he has personal faith in the candidate and asks nothing but good government. The situation varies with the character of individuals.

In the legislature I sponsored a bill strengthening the right of various communities to have local-option elections on the sale of liquor within their boundaries. I imagine the report also is widespread that, personally, I am a teetotaler. Yet a tavern operator voluntarily sent a $25 donation to my campaign fund. His letter warmed my heart: 'You voted in a way to hurt my business, but I think you are on the level. I don't expect you to change your mind on my own problems because of this small contribution. Just keep on representing the public.'

This altruism contrasted with the attitude of the prominent citizen who told one of my friends he would send in a check amounting to 'at least $500' if I reversed my position on certain phases of the state gambling laws. It is scarcely to my credit that I spurned the offer.

Yet it is the system which is essentially wrong and not individual people. As long as public offices can be bought, ambitious and greedy men will try to buy them.

Political contributions are not deductible for tax purposes. The temptation frequently exists to look upon them as business expenditures. Instead of purchasing pine lumber or cases of pineapple, a man invests in a Senator or Governor. This expectation of return on an investment sullies the unselfish spirit of the minority of donors, who anticipate only integrity in office.

Even in our modest amphitheatre of a state legislature, the grim tendency to amortize investments often prevails. This was demonstrated by a recent telephone call which I received.

'Senator,' began the friendly voice on the line, 'we know it costs money to run for the Legislature. Our group would like to send you a check for $250 to help take care of some of your campaign expenses.'

'That would be fine,' I answered gratefully, 'but I think you are entitled to be told in advance that I am opposed to the bill you are sponsoring to change the state health laws.'

The voice hesitated, then mumbled a polite reply and the receiver clicked in my ear. I knew the $250 never would be forthcoming.

Can a candidate take a contribution and still defy the contributor's demands? Along with Maurine, I was offered a donation by a wealthy man with dairy holdings. Because she had put through the bill to legalize colored margarine, we decided that we had to turn down the donation or else never undertake such an advocacy in behalf of consumers again. We could not see ourselves going against the interests of a man whose money we had accepted. It seemed to us that the poet in old England was right when he said, 'He who takes the King's shilling must do the King's business.'

This is why gangsters and gamblers, barred from office themselves by public opinion, can gain great influence through financial favors. Honest views about government sometimes have so little to do with political donations that many people give money to both sides.

They don't care to be on the outs with any group which might ascend to power. I talked with a liquor salesman in one state who donated funds to opposing gubernatorial candidates.

'If I can't sell to the state liquor stores I'm out of business,' he explained. 'Making a campaign contribution is the way I keep in good standing.'

The Federal Hatch Act is supposed to restrict the annual expenditures of a party's national committee to $3,000,000. This sounds effective, but each major party has evaded the act simply by organizing satellite committees with high-sounding names. Through these subordinate groups the parties spend as much as they can collect.

Somewhere along the line, contributors will talk bluntly to party henchmen. A paper mill may hope to continue to dump chemical wastes in a navigable river where people swim and fish or even get their drinking supply. Truckers may want to forestall any discussion of highway mileage taxes. These talks may never reach the ears of the Presidential nominees, but the party 'wheels' will be thoroughly aware of obligations that eventually must be fulfilled.

The Hatch Act 'limits' a citizen to $5000 in campaign contributions to any committee or candidate during a year. This is avoided by a number of easy devices. After all, a baby qualifies as an individual. Infants in families have been known to make $5000 campaign donations before they left the bassinet. And the many separate committees with high-flown titles, such as War Veterans for Eisenhower or Business Men Behind Stevenson, always have been useful channels for receiving numerous different $5000 gratuities from the same person or family.

Seldom does anyone ever come to trial for violation of a Corrupt Practices statute. In some states it unquestionably is more risky to steal a crate of tomatoes than to steal a great election through illegal expenditures. One of the few prosecutions under an election law took place in 1951 in Maryland. John M. Jonkel, campaign manager for Senator John M. Butler, was fined $5000 for not revealing total campaign expenses.

Butler himself, however, continues to sit in the Senate until 1957, so any benefits from the crime of his manager are conveniently retained.

The compulsion to win in politics is mighty, and money often makes the difference between victory and defeat. This applies to issues as well as to candidates. Professor Winston W. Crouch, examining forty years of the initiative and referendum in California, has said that 'in most instances the old adage of politics that "the side which spends the most wins" has proven true.'

From my grandstand seat as a member of a State Senate, I have seen how easy it is for campaign spending to get completely out of control.

An election contest may begin modestly, with the rival candidates determined to keep free of heavy financial commitments. Then one contestant buys a number of billboards. The other decides he must retaliate with an 'orchid day' for the women voters in the district. The first candidate comes back with a TV program or thousands of matchbox covers carrying his picture. Entrant No. 1 retorts with an elaborate brochure sent through the mails.

By now the spending spree is on for fair. I have

watched a man, trapped on this kind of treadmill, sink $4000 in a campaign to win an office that would pay him $600 annual salary!

But what can be done to make it possible for those who govern us to enter office free of sinister obligations? Still more important, how can we know exactly to whom a specific candidate may be indebted financially?

Borrowing an idea which Theodore Roosevelt originated when he was President back in 1907, Senator Douglas of Illinois has suggested that political campaigns be paid for entirely by the government. 'The question is raised,' says he, 'as to whether it would not be cheaper and better to have campaign expenses borne directly by the public through taxes, rather than indirectly as now through favors.'

This suggestion, worthy though it is, collides with several difficulties. What about minor parties? Would they receive government financing, too? After all, the Republican party itself emerged from feeble beginnings to succeed the Whigs. Would this have been possible if the Whigs had been propped up by the Federal treasury?

Then the question of the primary election must be answered. In many states the primary is frequently more decisive than the general election. Would public financing go to any candidate who wanted his name on the ballot? And if it were not given under these universal terms, how could it be justified in the name of democracy and equality? What candidates would be excluded?

To make public financing of campaigns effective, a Presidential aspirant would have to be underwritten by the national exchequer the moment he announced his high ambitions. Otherwise, what good would it do to free the candidate of improper debts during the election race, if he already had secured the nomination with millions of dollars obtained from private sources? The corralling of party delegates is a costly matter. In 1948 Harold E. Stassen accused Thomas E. Dewey of spending $250,000 just to wrest Oregon's eight convention votes from him. And in 1952 the Eisenhower and Taft forces had invested innumerable times this sum by the time the G.O.P. delegates sat down in Chicago's Stockyard Arena.

All these corollary doubts must be resolved before the idea of public financing of political campaigns has a chance of adoption. And if the electorate is not ready for this drastic remedy, how can the present system of indiscriminate private financing of political contests be patrolled?

III

Congressional committees headed by Senator Guy Gillette of Iowa and Mike Mansfield of Montana have been studying this thorny problem for several years. So have legislative commissions in many of the states, including one in Oregon of which I am a member.

By combining the ideas of these various groups, we come up with a set of recommendations:

1. Extend Corrupt Practices laws to the primaries, which are far more crucial than the November elections in one-party states where Democrats or Republicans hold iron control.

2. Take off unrealistic ceiling limits on spending, which merely encourage evasion, but require that all donations above $50 be reported along with full information about the donor.

3. Demand reporting of expenditures before the election as well as afterward. The present clumsy method is like having blood tests after marriage.

4. Require all funds spent in a campaign to be funneled through one committee.

5. Make the candidate himself approve in writing acceptance of all contributions larger than $50. No more back-alley deals by campaign managers without his knowledge.

6. Take state election bureaus out of party politics and put them under Civil Service.

7. Close the loopholes governing campaign financing by corporations and labor unions.

8. Require strict auditing of all campaign books.

9. Take away any office that was won by fraud or illegal political expenditures.

Adoption of most of these foregoing proposals might modify the danger that campaign slush funds will decide who sits in the oak-and-leather chairs of governmental authority.

Senator Mansfield believes it particularly urgent that the details of campaign financing be revealed throughout an election. Yet is this precaution enough? The problem of money in elections is so fraught with peril to democracy that we must make sure we are getting to the heart of the problem.

Mansfield points out that a candidate may hesitate to accept donations from the underworld and other evil sources if this might be found out by the voters. A searching audit also would satisfy an objection by former President Herbert Hoover, who announced recently that he was disturbed about 'the lack of accountability over huge expenditures in these political campaigns.'

The American people want their public officials to be their own bosses, not men pulled by invisible financial strings. A Gallup poll has shown that a majority of voters would be willing to put up $5 apiece each year to provide the sole support of the political party which they favor. This could be one way of keeping large chunks of tainted money from corrupting government.

My wife and I have come to the conclusion that our whole process of government is degraded by the large sums of money now spent to elect candidates to office. To begin with, the nominee often does not campaign in the accepted sense of the word. He is 'merchandised.' This will be handled by a plush advertising agency which receives as a fee 15 per cent of the funds in his political treasury.

One day the advertising firm may be promoting brassieres, soap, or a new auto polish. The next day its copy writers, artists, and executives are deciding what will 'sell' a candidate for the United States Senate. Elaborate and costly public-opinion polls are taken. Sensitive areas in the mind of the electorate are explored. The advertising agency then advises the candidate what line of attack will win votes. The prescribed remedy for victory may be an indictment of his opponent's patriotism. It may be a suggestion that all drafted soldiers be demobilized immediately. It could be promotion of the candidate's public meetings with girl torch singers or a hill-billy band.

What is right or what is in the public interest rarely, if ever, decides these copy conferences. The candidate for the Senate is just another piece of merchandise to

be put across in the realm of opinion. Even nominees
for the Oregon Legislature have to be sure they contract
for billboard space well in advance of election day.
Otherwise they may not be merchandised properly.
These billboards make no mention of what the candidate will do once he takes his seat in the legislature.
They merely hammer his name into the public sub-
conscious.

Indeed, unbridled financing of elections has imperiled the whole Jeffersonian concept of 'one man, one
vote.' Can a well-heeled citizen or wealthy corporation
use unlimited financial power to influence the votes of
all the public? This was hardly a threat in Jefferson's
time. It is a grave menace today when millions of
dollars are spent competing for the decision at the ballot
box. Jefferson relied on his personal letters, but
Judge Samuel Leibowitz withdrew from the 1953 New
York City Mayoralty race because he was told a 'winning campaign fund would have to contain nearly
$1,000,000.'

There must be further focus, too, on the person who
seeks to have public officials in his debt. Why should he
escape scrutiny? Edward Rowland Sill wrote in 'The
Fool's Prayer':

> *Earth bears no balsam for mistakes;*
> *Men crown the knave, and scourge the tool*
> *That did his will . . .*

Seated in the small amphitheater of the Oregon Legislature, we are well aware when the prior commitment
of campaign funds has preordained a certain outcome
on an important bill. It gives us an uncomfortable feeling. 'I'd like to vote with you,' an essentially honest

Senator said to me, 'but that fellow opposing this bill made a generous contribution to my campaign. I'm afraid I'm hooked.'

I have mentioned the glaring loophole in Oregon's state tax laws which permits real-estate firms to escape payment of the corporation excise tax. A struggling mama-and-papa grocery store may pay the tax, but not a firm owning millions of dollars worth of real-estate, just so long as 95 per cent of its income results from property rentals. Frequent efforts to plug the loophole have failed in the House of Representatives. We often have wondered if any connection exists between these failures and substantial donations to political campaigns by real-estate interests.

It is our opinion that there will not be truly free government in America—at the state, national, or local level—until campaign spending is rigidly controlled. In fact, why should a politician ever take a bribe when a donation to his next race for office is so much simpler—and so much more legal?

In nearly all mayoralty campaigns the people in 'the know' can predict which candidate will open up the town to prostitution, slot machines, and thousand-dollar poker hands in card rooms. It will be the candidate whose funds for radio, TV, and signboards originate in mysterious sources that never are clearly defined or understood. By the use of clever propaganda, the votes of thousands of God-fearing people can be influenced by money dredged up out of the underworld.

And, in higher echelons of policy, could there be a connection between utility-magnate contributions to political campaigns and Federal decisions to abandon valuable natural resources to private exploitation?

The British have limited what can be spent in a race for Parliament and they make the penalty for violation a denial of the right 'to speak and vote in the House of Commons.' We shall have to come to this eventually if we do not want governmental policies to be literally for sale, like baubles in a showcase.

Unwieldy though it might be to administer, Teddy Roosevelt's bygone suggestion may be the only possible remedy. Let the Federal treasury finance campaigns for national office and let state general funds pay for campaigns aimed toward the governorship and the state legislature. Operation of this system could be awkward and difficult, but it would prevent elections that are decided by slush funds rather than merit.

It is easy for some people to charge that trade unions are spending enormous sums in elections. Yet the Taft-Hartley Act has fastened tight hobbles on labor in this respect. It can donate to candidates for Federal office only 'free' funds which have been raised among members on a voluntary basis. No law inhibits a corporation from paying an officer a fat bonus, which then is passed on to some candidate who carries the corporation's flag and water bucket in the halls of government. In the 1952 campaign the entire Oregon State Federation of Labor spent only $4916 in behalf of candidates and causes which it favored. This was less than the Republican party spent in just one lumber-industry county of comparatively modest population.

The bespectacled Rough Rider, who was our nation's twenty-sixth President, never looked farther into the future than when he warned that powerful corporate interests might dominate government by exercising a monopoly over political campaign contributions.

– 11 –

THEY NEVER GO BACK TO

POCATELLO

In the dusk of evening I swung down from my Pullman in the Union Pacific's streamlined City of Portland at Pocatello and picked my way across the tracks, while the yellow diesel-electric locomotive was being serviced with fuel and lubricating oil.

Idaho's dark sagebrush uplands bulked like battlements above the sprawling brick station. At the ticket office I went through the local telephone directory once, and then I glanced up nervously at the sound of couplers bumping in the yards.

'Looking for someone, mister?' asked a lanky man with a green eyeshade behind the grille of the window. 'Maybe I can help you.'

I told him that I wanted to phone a friend of mine who had been a United States Senator from Idaho until a few years back. I once had gone fishing with the Senator and I hoped to say hello to him.

'Heck, mister,' said the Union Pacific station agent,

'I ain't seen him since he got licked for re-election. Knew him pretty well, too. Used to fix up his tickets for him. But he don't live here any more. Those guys never come back to Pocatello.'

Idaho citizens in general have decided that neither do they come back to Twin Falls, Boise, or Coeur d'Alene. Nor is this situation confined to Idaho. Men sent to Congress by Casper, Salt Lake City, Los Angeles, Des Moines, Charleston, and innumerable other places have also absented themselves permanently from the localities they formerly represented in the Senate and House of the national government.

It is one of the ironies of American politics that men who have been clogging the *Congressional Record* with tales of the glories and blessings of their constituencies take repulse at the polls as the signal never to look on those constituencies again.

On defeat, they vanish from local ken as completely as Ichabod Crane. Occasionally these vanquished politicians do not even return to crate the family possessions, trusting this chore to the impersonal hands of a moving crew.

Idaho, ribbed by lofty ranges and white-riffled rivers, has magnificent attractions, but evidently not for the individuals who have spoken for Idaho in the Congress of the United States. Three Idaho ex-Senators and three Idaho ex-Representatives still live, and some of them have roamed the continent—managing the Tennessee Valley Authority, constructing housing projects in Alaska, teaching in Ohio. These places are a far piece from the state which once hallowed them with Congressional authority.

Practically every state—especially states in the Far

West and on the Middle-Western prairies—has lost
former members of the Federal House and Senate
through self-imposed exile. The exiles are an impressive
tribe. They count four warriors even from sparsely
settled Nevada. They include such formidable figures as
Elmer Benson, ex-Governor and ex-Senator from Minnesota and Henry F. Ashurst, for 28 years a Senator from
Arizona.

This would seem to be entirely a Federal problem.
After all, the statesmen disappear from their home states
only when their Federal tenure is at an end. Yet, peculi-
arly enough, it is even more a dilemma for the states in
general and for state government in particular.

There goes on continually a sluicing off of many of
the most able people in state politics. The process involves three distinct stages: (1) the man or woman of
appeal at the polls quits his position in state government to seek a seat in the Federal Congress; (2) eventually he or she is separated by the voters from the Congressional seat; (3) the defeated member of Congress
stays on in Washington, D. C., or some other distant
place and never returns to the home state.

This drain of talent never stops. It is perennial. The
Governor or State Senator asks himself why he should
be struggling with such matters as a new cell block for
the penitentiary when he could be deciding the more
exotic issues of war and peace, wire tapping, and FBI
appropriations.

The Governor's wife asks questions, too. Part of the
lure of the national capital is unquestionably social,
which means the distaff side of the politician's family.
Standing in the reception line at a typical hotel in a
state capital city of perhaps 35,000 population, the

hometown girl whom the Governor married long ago
has visions of the Sulgrave Club, of tea at the White
House, of cocktails at the British embassy, of a bearded
ambassador from a strange land gravely kissing her
manicured hand.

With these notions in mind, the wife of the Governor
comes to look upon the state capital as pretty small
potatoes. Why should her talents be limited to this
cramped social domain? Should she not operate in a
wider, more glittering realm? Accompanying her husband to a potluck supper of the Pitchfork Union suddenly seems drab and unglamorous, when she might be
gracefully declining hors d'oeuvre proffered by the
servants of European nobility.

Such pressures few politicians can resist, for they frequently are husbands first and public servants second.
If mamma wants to go to Washington, then state government abruptly becomes less important to the Governor than Federal government. State's rights are
urgent, but only in political speeches. Mamma's rights—
and wishes—are with him at mealtime, in the boudoir,
and at many places in between.

So he heads for Washington, and state government
has lost a capable leader. Worst of all, he never comes
back.

II

After nearly three decades as a Senator from Arizona,
Henry Ashurst told his colleagues that he would return
'to the starry stillness of an Arizona desert night, the
scarlet glories of her blooming cactus, the petrified
forest which leafed through its green millenniums and
put on immortality seven thousand years ago.'

Yet Senator Ashurst did not get farther west permanently than the Wardman Park Hotel in Washington, D. C., and the closest that he approached to the petrified forest was the fringe of foliage between the Wardman Park and the busy traffic along Connecticut Avenue.

In choosing to make his full-time residence in the country's capital, the Arizona statesman was following the standard practice. His decision was not abnormal in any respect.

The march of political talent from the states to Washington is all in one direction. And if the defeated politician does not remain in Washington, he generally picks out some sanctuary that is equally distant from the state where he got his political start.

Most of these storm cellars were not dug on the spur of the moment. Their occupants thought about them during many years of statesmanship. 'I always realized,' said Professor Burton L. French of Ohio's Miami University, who had been Congressman for twenty-six years from the forests of Northern Idaho, 'that persons in elective political offices are subject to shifts of sentiment. With this idea, over the years I kept in close touch with educational work. I felt that when my work in Congress would be over I should go to some university faculty as a professor of government.'

'My inclination and desire is naturally to return to my home city of Twin Falls, Idaho,' admitted Addison Smith, another ex-Idaho Congressman, 'but as I know of no way to be profitably occupied there, and am doing very well in Washington, D. C., I must forego the pleasure of being among my Idaho friends.'

Jonathan Bourne, Jr., first Senator to be elected by a direct vote of the people, never went back to Oregon, because he frankly confessed that Washington, D. C., seemed 'a whole lot more like home.'

Some of the reasons for such a situation were hinted at by Senator Estes Kefauver of Tennessee, when he said that 'people here on Capitol Hill, particularly those from the far-off Western states, are away from home so long that they are in danger of losing touch with their constituents. They get in an ivory tower, so to speak.' And Representative W. R. Poage, of Texas, suggested that members of Congress be paid 'a regular mileage and regular per diem,' so they can go back to their districts more frequently. He is opposed to the present system, under which Congressman receives twenty cents a mile for approximately one trip a year, but the rest of the time must pungle up for his fare. He believes that most people think Senators and Representatives get the twenty-cent rate for every trip. 'It is embarrassing to return home,' says Poage, 'and have the folks think, "Well, he is just grafting on the Government." '

Senator Bourne, a rich man, simply conceded he had more friends in Washington than in the state which had sent him there. But many Congressmen stay on in the national capital because it offers greater possibilities of paying the grocery bill. Before the recent upping of their salaries and a generous expense allowance, a lot of them complained that they ended up their political careers in the red because of money they had to pay out of their own pockets for clerk hire.

Some Congressional rejects get Government plums, others crab apples. At the end of eight years in the House, Bernard J. Gehrmann, a Progressive from Wisconsin, went to work for the Farm Security Administration at $3800 annually. On the other hand, Harry H.

Schwartz, New Deal Democrat from Wyoming, became a member of the National Mediation Board at $10,000, after his defeat for re-election to the Senate in 1942.

Seats on numerous boards and commissions call for compensation approximating that of a Senator or Congressman. 'If you get trimmed while your party is in power and you've been regular,' observes one ex-Senator, 'you can stay in Washington with your standard of living undisturbed. But if the other crowd is in the saddle, you probably will have to move into a clerk's office and a smaller house.'

After Oklahoma's voters ended the tenure of Josh Lee as their Senator in 1942, President Roosevelt appointed the silver-tongued New Dealer to the Civil Aeronautics Board, where he continued to enjoy a senatorial pay level. A former Democratic Senator from Nevada, seventy-three-year-old Charles B. Henderson, became chairman of the RFC. Bennett Champ Clark, turned down for a third senatorial term, was able to avoid a return to Missouri when his erstwhile colleague, Harry Truman, appointed him to the Court of Appeals for the District of Columbia.

Bountifulness to repudiated legislators does not flow only from the White House. Senators and Representatives reserve a tender spot in their hearts for defeated comrades. 'There, but for the grace of God, go I' is a prevalent Congressional emotion whenever the election-day wreckage is inventoried.

Wall Doxey, sergeant at arms of the Senate under the Democrats, was once a Representative and later a Senator from Mississippi. A clerk of the House, South Trimble, served three terms as a Congressman from Kentucky. Melvin Mass, former Representative from a

St. Paul district, became chief investigator of the Naval Affairs Committee on which he sat as a member. Other ex-legislators occupy liaison and legal posts on Capitol Hill.

Lobbying, of course, offers a snug refuge for many powerful Congressional figures whose constituents have tired of their services. They represent every element from the CIO to the Republican National Committee. Some merely are counselors-at-law, speaking for such clients as choose to knock on their glass-paneled doors. A few of the friends of the late Robert M. La Follette, Jr., one of the great luminaries of Wisconsin politics, believe that his tragic suicide may have stemmed from the fact that he stayed on in the national capital as a representative of various private clients, rather than returning to Wisconsin to carry on the political fight against McCarthyism and other forces traditionally abhorrent to the La Follette family. Despondency may have followed this retreat.

Yet to return to one's home state after a defeat at the polls could mean starting all over again at the bottom of the political staircase. It would be tantamount to Johnny Mize or Joe Di Maggio beginning once more in sandlot or high-school baseball. What would a man who had been State Senator, Governor, Congressman, and U. S. Senator think in his inner thoughts if he had to struggle to be even a State Senator for a second time?

It is easier to stay on in Washington, where the rewards total up to more financially and perhaps even more politically. After the Democrats had retired him from the United States Senate, John A. Danaher of Connecticut became a Congressional lieutenant on the staff of the Republican National Committee at $20,000 a year. When the Republicans eventually came back into national power, President Eisenhower named Danaher to be a Federal judge. Remaining in Washington had paid off far more durably than a return to Connecticut possibly could have promised.

William A. Ekwall, Republican Representative from Portland, Oregon, delivered a speech telling his constituents that even if they defeated him, he wished nothing better than to return and dwell among them for the rest of his days. They took him at his word. He now lives in Bronxville, New York, having been appointed by President Franklin D. Roosevelt as a minority member of the United States Customs Court.

Albert G. Simms of Albuquerque, New Mexico, was one of the Congressmen who did go home after defeat. He thought the reason he went back to the wide open spaces may have been that he was only a one-termer. 'It is my observation,' he said, 'that some members of Congress who have had long tenure of office gradually lose their contact with the home people, and so Washington then becomes home for them.'

The late Senator Charles L. McNary of Oregon used to claim that strong psychological factors worked to keep a man from returning to the constituency which repudiated him. 'As he walks down the street,' said McNary, a shrewd observer of politics, 'he thinks each person he passes is one of the votes that beat him. In addition, Washington has an intoxication for many people. You rub elbows with the mighty. You feel important. It is not easy to buy a ticket to Podunk after being at the center of things. One's self-esteem takes an awful drop.'

III

But the tendency to rush to Washington—and then never to return—adds up to bad news for state government.

Probably the Governor or State Senator is right who decides that his political talents, having been fully developed, are needed at the level of government where the most important decisions are to be taken. These, of course, are decisions in the international sphere. Yet, after defeat, is he justified in staying away forever from the state which gave him his start?

In Canada, I have observed, there is great flexibility between the national and provincial spheres of government. It is not uncommon for a member of the Federal Parliament to retire as an MP in order to try to rehabilitate his party's fortunes within the province. Then, if successful, he becomes the provincial Premier, a position comparable in authority and duties to the Governor of a state. Many Premiers and cabinet ministers in the ten provinces of Canada are men who once sat under the soaring Gothic spire of the Peace Tower in Ottawa, where the national House of Commons convenes. Canadians do not regard a withdrawal from the Federal to the provincial echelon of government as at all out of the ordinary.

This has happened so rarely in the United States that an exception only serves to prove the rule. James F. Byrnes was U. S. Senator from South Carolina, Supreme Court Justice, and Secretary of State. Now he is the Governor of South Carolina. Yet this occurred not as part of a traditional political career, but because Byrnes broke completely with the Democratic Party, which had sponsored these high honors in his behalf.

Yet Byrnes was willing to go back to his home state to live, and for this he deserves a measure of credit. The capital city of Columbia (pop. 86,914) was not too small for him after the glamour of Washington and the chancellories of Europe.

Few other politicians follow this route. Once Mon Wallgren had been counted out for re-election as Governor of the state of Washington, he took off for Palm Springs, California. An ex-Georgia Congressman became executive vice-president of the Air Transport Association, an ex-Virginia Congressman became head of the American Plant Food Council, and an ex-Massachusetts Congressman became counsel for Transcontinental & Western Airlines. Naturally, these tempting positions required the presence of the former statesmen in Washington, D. C. No retreat to state politics for them!

Once a man or woman has left the State Legislature or the gubernatorial chambers for a fling at Congress, he or she is gone for good. In this essential, state government is worse off than the minor leagues in baseball. The minors train recruits for the major leagues. But after a baseball player has finished his period of usefulness in the big show, he usually totes his ailing arm or slowing legs back to the Pacific Coast League or International Association for a few seasons of moderate usefulness.

This almost never takes place in politics. After a politician has left the state capitol building for Congress, he is seen no more at his old haunts—except possibly on a fleeting outdoor trip to catch Steelhead or Rainbows with other assorted VIP's. And because he fails to return to the home state to make his residence, he is not even available to advise the next generation. The constant loss of talent and experience does state government no good in the long run.

Yet perhaps Harry S. Truman may be setting an example which others, some time, will choose to emulate. In all the welter of abuse directed at Truman, it is forgotten that he went back to Independence, Missouri, while Herbert Hoover went not to Palto Alto, California, but to the Waldorf Towers on New York's Park Avenue.

Harry Truman was not too proud or too big for his britches to return to his home state. All the abuse by the Jenners and Brownells and McCarthys cannot erase this bright spot from the ex-President's shield! He was loyal enough to Independence to go back there to make his home.

– 12 –

WHERE DO WE GO

FROM HERE?

I

PROFESSOR Charles McKinley of Reed College, a small school of extraordinarily high academic standards near Portland, has told us that the position in Oregon politics of the Neubergers, husband and wife, reminds him of a student who inquired how he had fared in mid-term examinations.

'Nelson,' said McKinley to his pupil, 'I'm putting you first of all the flunks.'

'That's the way the Neubergers stand in Oregon,' analyzed the political science teacher. 'You're tops among Democrats but the Democrats have been flunking in Oregon for many decades. Where do you folks go from here?'

Because our party has been a minority so long in Oregon, do we have a freedom of choice? At the crest of FDR's popularity, when even such strongholds of Republicanism as Kansas and Nebraska and South Dakota were sending Democrats to the Senate, Oregon remained a redoubt of the Grand Old Party. Many Oregon editors regard Republicanism as synonymous with godliness. They would sooner walk a tightrope strung between Mount Everest and K_2 than mutter a good word about a Democrat. If the Republicans become involved in a scandal—as is sometimes the case—then this is merely trouble in Paradise and the less said about it the better.

What is the future for members of the political minority in such a situation? Surely the dilemma which Maurine and I face must be similar to that confronting other men and women in politics in the one-party states of the Union. What does a Republican do in Georgia or Mississippi? Chart a course, if you dare, for a Democrat in Maine or Vermont. Talk all that you will about the two-party system, but it fails to exist at the state or Congressional level in nearly half the states of these United States.

During the 1952 Presidential campaign, Oregon Republicans orated frequently for restoration of the two-party system in Washington, D. C. But the most essential portion of this appeal, in their minds, was its limitation to Washington, D. C. They made it abundantly clear that the two-party system ought to be stopped at the Oregon state line, just like the California fruit fly and illegal Mexican immigrants.

Should either of the Neubergers run for the Governorship or the United States Senate? Undoubtedly, one or the other of us could win the seat in the Federal House of Representatives from the Portland district. Even our adversaries concede this. But would such a victory, impressive though it might seem, restore genuine political competition in Oregon? I doubt it.

An embryonic Congressman has little or no genuine

authority. Perhaps he can get the floor to deliver a speech late in the afternoon, with few present except the acting Speaker and the shorthand reporters, who are without freedom of choice in the matter. He is lost in the hurly-burly of 435 members. He must run for re-election every two years, with his return to office eternally in doubt.

Actually, the only positions that promise hope of reviving the cherished two-party system in a one-party state are the gubernatorial chair or a seat in the Senate. These posts are statewide in sovereignty. The term is sufficiently long to give a person a chance to show his mettle. He can bring up genuine issues. A forum is provided of enough prestige and influence to reach voters shielded even by unfair segments of the press.

Yet does a citizen sound in mind and body deliberately set out to defy the odds in a one-party state? Why not roll with the punches and stay away from the in-fighting? What befalls a Democrat who seeks to become Governor of Oregon or one of its two Senators on Capitol Hill? I shall go into some clinical details because the pattern must be identical in other one-party states.

The Democrat is immediately opposed by a state administration which has purposely kept the State Police, a substantial portion of the State Liquor Monopoly, and other bureaus from being placed under Civil Service. Most of the thirty-six county courthouses are Republican in allegiance. Civil Service likewise has fared poorly in this sphere. A ready horde of party workers, financed by the taxpayers, is at the disposal of the Republican party to help persuade the taxpayers that they should continue to 'vote 'er straight.' Yet I am convinced that many state employees, at heart, want a change in Oregon.

Among Oregon's daily newspapers, a few papers in medium-sized communities might back a Democrat for major office, although this is by no means assured. Yet on these hinterland dailies, at least, all-out indorsement of Republicans is not automatic. But most of the state's press can be depended upon to assign its editorial pages to perpetuation of one-party rule. Some of these pages —and on famous papers, too—even refuse to print letters-to-the-editor that call attention to holes in the public records of prominent Republicans. Syndicated columnists are similarly censored toward the same end.

It must be pointed out, in equity, that a majority of working reporters and many executives try to be impartial in handling political affairs in the news columns. They attempt to give all sides an even break. This was not always the situation in Oregon. Until the advent of Palmer Hoyt as managing editor of the *Oregonian,* the bulk of the state's press filled nearly all pages except sports and classified advertising with Republican propaganda. Hoyt, who since has become the crusading editor of the *Denver Post,* dug a deep moat between editorial-page opinion and the news content of his paper. The separation has been fairly effective. Unfortunately, Hoyt was denied the authority to insist that endorsement of political candidates be based on merit rather than on fealty to the Republican Party.

'The way some papers have to endorse all Republicans willy-nilly, regardless of worth, character or ability,' said Hoyt to me, 'is about as silly as backing all candidates six feet tall or those who wear blue shirts or Stetson hats. It doesn't make sense.'

Other obstacles imperil a minority adventurer in a one-party state. If normal campaign expenditures are available, the Republican nominee for the governorship or Senate will have a fund of about $75,000 to spend promoting his candidacy. In addition, the Republican State Central Committee and affiliated groups will disburse approximately $250,000 heralding Republican candidates in general.

The Democratic nominee in Oregon, by contrast, will have at his disposal a prevailing minority-party exchequer of something in the neighborhood of $15,000. The Democratic State Committee and satellite organizations may raise another $25,000 to spend on the promotion of all candidates on the ticket—although this would be far beyond standard expectations.

What impact does this preponderance of Republican campaign funds have on the conduct of an election race? It means that the Democratic nominee for the state Capitol or national Capitol must reach most voters by word of mouth. He has to drive from town to town, from farm to farm, from railroad roundhouse to logging-camp bunkhouse, from garment factory to college campus. He will have to be on the move from dawn until well after midnight in order to contact enough people to have even an outside chance for victory.

As the exhausted Democrat wheels along Oregon's miles and miles of trunk highways and secondary roads, he will see at strategic intervals a coterie of billboards blaring the name of his Republican opponent. He may turn on the car radio. He will hear lively one-minute jingles, to the tune of *Clementine* or *Alouette,* telling the listener why the Republican candidate is 'fine, fine, fine, just the fellow to keep things in line. . . .'

It could be that the Democratic candidate will pull over to the side of the highway to let a high-speed motor caravan rumble past. This will be the Republican candidate and his retinue. A chartered bus may contain speech writers, advertising-copy specialists, public relations counselors, and one or two privileged court jesters to put the candidate at ease. Another bus might transport a brass band. There also will be a sound truck to announce to all within blaring earshot that the Republican nominee has come to town. There may even be souvenirs for the first 500 arrivals at the party rally that evening.

Of course, the voters will not learn until after the votes are counted—and only hazily, if then—the sources of the vast amount of money to pay for all this. Too late, the electorate may decide what obligations in the form of public policy and legislation go hand-in-hand with acceptance of such large sums for the financing of political promotion and campaigning.

What choice does this formidable stacking of the odds leave the man or woman of genuine political convictions in the one-party state? The Florida Republican, the Maine Democrat, the Georgia Republican, the Oregon Democrat, do they fold their tents and silently steal away, like Longfellow's furtive Arabs?

Maurine and I are glad we have made the fight in the Legislature against the big, overpowering majority. But the challenge still remains of the harder, sterner tests that lie beyond. When we talk about this challenge, Maurine reminds me of one of our favorite friends, the late Colonel Denny La Nauze of the Royal Canadian Mounted Police. We shall never forget him. He was a jolly Irishman with an abiding love of the human race.

As a young Inspector in the Mounties, Denny was called to headquarters at Edmonton by his Superintendent. Two Catholic missionaries had disappeared in the white solitudes of the Northwest Territories. They were two years overdue at Fort Norman, on the Mackenzie River. Not a trace of them had been located. The Superintendent suspected foul play by stone-age Eskimos along the Arctic Ocean. Yet it was a suspicion without a clue. Furthermore, the Northwest Territories were nearly half the size of the United States. It would be like trying to find a particular pebble in a stone quarry.

Contrary to legend, the famous Mounties never are told, "Don't come back until you get your man.' The Superintendent said to La Nauze:

'Think the odds are too great for one person, Denny? Shall I send a big patrol?'

Our old friend replied, 'When do I start, sir—and alone?'

This is the tale that Maurine calls to mind again when we talk about the difficulty of bucking the one-party state in scenic Oregon.

II

We have no desire to be in the position, ever, of not choosing to go back to Pocatello. Our 'Pocatello' is the state where we both were born—Oregon. This is the place where we want to live for the rest of our lives.

For this reason the Governorship is the most tempting when we mention higher political goals. The Governor's job is inside his home state. In addition, our public service thus far has been in the Legislature, and this is an adjunct of the duties of the Governor's office. We would be dealing with the same issues that had occupied us as legislators. And we would be dealing with them in Oregon. We never would have to decide the momentous question of whether to go back to 'Pocatello.' We would be there all the time.

Yet we frequently think that in spite of all these compelling arguments the truly urgent need for liberal-minded people is in the Federal Congress, especially in the U. S. Senate.

This need stems from the rise of what our friend Palmer Hoyt refers to as 'mccarthyism.' Hoyt is careful to use a small 'm' because he considers mccarthyism a national trend of great danger and not merely the personal propensity of one individual politician.

Here is how Hoyt defines mccarthyism:

'It is the totalitarian device of making the charge more important than the law, the evidence, the verdict or the trial.'

The practice of mccarthyism has gotten out of hand in American life, particularly in the Congress. A Senator can charge the winner of the Nobel Peace prize with being 'a living lie' and a front man for traitors. Another Senator can indict the loyalty of an ex-President and the patriotism of innumerable cabinet members. As Palmer Hoyt has pointed out, the charge frequently is an end in and of itself. No direct evidence supports the charge, but is that important? The mud has been hurled. Some of it has stuck. Let the accused prove his own innocence. Mccarthyism reverses Anglo-Saxon standards of justice.

Once the courts were the final test of the loyalty of Americans. Now it is public statements by politicians. Were these politicians to retreat 150 years in time and space, we need no creative imagination to hear them questioning the patriotism of General George Washington because he placed great trust in his old comrade-in-arms, Benedict Arnold.

Today, men of mediocre ability have been able to develop dazzling political careers for themselves through the device of leveling indiscriminate charges of 'Communism' against all who criticize their views. Democracy to these people has become principally a matter of anti-Communism. And even in this field, they often substitute the word for the deed. Ironic though it may seem, men who have fought against Communists on the field of battle have had their patriotism challenged by men who oppose Communism only with oratory. The affirmative defense of basic freedoms has been abandoned in favor of mere hostility to Communism. Were Jefferson to have composed the Declaration of Independence in such an atmosphere, he would have been under pressure to jettison 'life, liberty and the pursuit of happiness' in order to make way for one more denunciation of George III.

'If a particular cause is worthy of support, it does not cease to merit support because men we disapprove support it,' Henry Steele Commager has written in *The New York Times Magazine*. 'For if bad support could damage a good cause, then all that would be needed to tarnish the Declaration of Independence or destroy the Constitution would be the endorsement of these documents by the Communist Party.'

Yet even at the state level, in Oregon, we have many politicians who assail ideas or organizations because one or two unworthy individuals may have attached themselves to these groups. Let a Communist criticize the sales tax or plead for civil rights, and *ipso facto* all people affiliated with these advocacies become suspect. Some private-utility groups have emphasized the fact that Communists favor the high Federal dam at Hell's Canyon on the Snake River. What does this do to the Corps of Army Engineers, who also favored the dam in their $5,000,000 study known as *The 308 Report*? Guilt by association yields many weird results.

Absurd though such reckless charges may seem, they make men timid and hesitant. Who is to blame them? Families must eat. To be denounced as 'subversive' now, if only by the most unscrupulous politician, is to place in peril the daily bread. Few can afford this risk. When unsupported charges of Communist sympathies are directed at men like General George C. Marshall and ex-President Harry Truman, these people have the resources with which to defend their reputations. Such bastions are not always available to the average individual.

In a mountain valley of British Columbia, where glacial creeks foamed through stands of lodgepole pine, a Mountie traveling with Maurine and me asked why the wartime Soviet espionage ring had become such a political issue in the United States. He pointed out that the same spy ring had been extremely active in Canada. It was trapped by the Mounties, with the aid of the Russian code-clerk Gouzenko. 'But the presence of these spies in Canada never was used in parliament against the Mackenzie King government,' said our policeman friend.

As a faint glow of the aurora borealis gleamed in the night sky, I explained to the Mountie that certain politicians in the United States could avoid grappling with questions like taxes, farm parity, the cost of living, and conservation of resources if they were successful in mak-

ing it appear that their political adversaries were dis-
loyal to the United States.

I am not sure that the Mountie, an unpolitical individual, ever really understood my explanation, which
probably was inadequate, at best. Rigidly disciplined to
acceptance of a stern code of loyalty and duty, I am con-
fident it was beyond his conception that anyone would
deliberately sacrifice national unity on such an issue as
foreign spies merely to win votes.

Americans of every generation have produced new
ideas for strengthening government and making it more
responsive to the popular will. The Emancipation Proc-
lamation was a new idea, and so were the Forest Reserve
Act and the Social Security laws.

Mccarthyism has had the effect of choking off the flow
of creative suggestions. People become fearful that inno-
vations will be equated as tantamount to Communism.
After all, the Oregon Legislature of 1901 denounced
Gifford Pinchot and other pioneer foresters as 'untried
theorists.' The term 'Communism' was not widely
known at the time, or it undoubtedly would have been
used.

On a recent morning, just before a trip onto the high
plateau of eastern Oregon, I received a letter from a
ranch housewife in Deschutes County. Her name was
Mary Katherine Swearingen. This is what her letter
asked:

'Isn't there some way of finding a fair price for farmers' products without limiting their output? The re-
stricting of acreage works the most hardship on the
small rancher. All this talk of supports with acreage
allotments makes me think of a balloon with a given
amount of air in it. You can only make it bigger in one

part by squeezing it in another. My husband and I have
been talking about the idea of combining a food-stamp
plan with the sort of plan they have in Canada for helping the children. I am sure there must be very few families in America which couldn't use more and better food
for their children . . ."

I thought a lot about Mrs. Swearingen's letter. I also
reviewed the Family Allowances system which Maurine
and I had seen in operation during our many writing
trips to Canada. Under this system, the Canadian government pays to all mothers a certain sum of money each
month for every child under the age of 16. The sum
goes to families as a matter of right. There is no means
test. Canadians qualify if they have children. The payments commence at birth. They range from $5 to $8 a
child, monthly.

Family Allowances have resulted in increased sales of
pablum, eggs, milk, butter, fruit juices, and other foods
of importance to the health of children. The program
costs approximately $295,000,000 in Canada. It would
require $3,000,000,000 annually in the United States—a
huge sum, I admit, but perhaps a better way of using
our agricultural surpluses than to let them rot in fields
or warehouses.

I asked several of my friends what they thought of my
proposing this idea when I spoke at a banquet in the
wheat country above the Columbia River Gorge. They
cogitated a few moments. Finally, one of them said, 'It'll
just get you called a Communist or Socialist or something like that—especially because it comes from another
country. Better forget it.'

The others concurred with reluctance.

I thought about this situation for a long time. The

176 ADVENTURES IN POLITICS

fears of my friends had given me pause. Yet what else was America but a series of new ideas? After all, the Northwest Ordinance and the Bill of Rights might never have been written if men always had been afraid. What if James Madison had been dissuaded?

Family Allowances could not be considered in the same category as these immortal charters of freedom, but bonuses to families with children might be a more wholesome way of grappling with dunes of butterfat than allowing it to spoil in storage. Would my hero, Thomas Jefferson, have been frightened out of venturing a bold proposition of government?

I am no more valorous than the next politician but I at last went through with my plan to propose Family Allowances. Sure enough, somebody did denounce me as a Socialist. Maurine, however, recommended the reply on my part that America's biggest capitalists had invested $9,000,000,000 in Canada while Family Allowances have been in effect. This seemed to her answer enough. I thought so, too.

III

Like all other things in life, politics can be both encouraging and extremely discouraging. I recollect the leader of the longshoremen who admitted my 100 per cent voting record in the Legislature on labor bills and social legislation, but declared his union could not possibly back me because I had expressed doubt, in answer to a question from the floor, whether we should share atomic secrets with the Soviet Union. His antagonistic attitude may have been due to Communist leanings, but this could not be said of the clergyman who conceded our full agreement on moral problems such as gambling

and vice, yet advised worshipers to vote against me because of an article my wife had written for the magazine section of the *Oregonian* about the experiences of
a statuesque ballet dancer who posed nude for local
artists.

Yet these rather narrow approaches to the task of
choosing one's official spokesman in the Legislature have
not been typical. The average citizen is a more generous
and understanding creature than some of his so-called
'betters' like to believe.

Ours is not a state with a large Jewish population.
There are approximately 10,000 Jews among 1,600,000
inhabitants. This may be the reason that I have encountered virtually no religious prejudice. During all my
campaigns for office many acquaintances, Jew and Gen-
tile alike, warned me of the anti-Semitism which might
lessen my chances. I know that some people believe such
feeling is rampant all over America. I am no sociologist
and cannot assay the truth of this, but I do know the
fact that I am a Jew did not keep me from heading my
party's ticket in 1946, in 1948, and again in 1952.

Only once did I run into an active outburst of anti-
Semitism. At a pension rally a man with loud stentorian
voice assailed Jews in general and me in particular.
Angry and tense, I was about to jump to my feet in answer, when a leader in the pension movement, a man
over seventy with a fine leonine head, got up and said
very quietly:

'I figure we're all Americans, everyone of us here. Our
friend Neuberger found that out when he was serving
in Army uniform in the war we've only recently ended.
I found it out in the Spanish-American War.'

And Charley Townsend sat down.

I am sure the incident reacted to my benefit. Afterward practically the entire audience lined up to shake my hand. They were obviously embarrassed for fear my feelings had been hurt. I know some of them redoubled their efforts to make certain I carried that neighborhood—which I did.

To be perpetually in the minority is frustrating, but only if one shuts his eyes to history. What if there had been no legislative minority in 1901 to take to the ultimate tribune of the people the Legislature's memorial against the proposed Forest Reserve system? Without such minorities in Oregon and elsewhere in the West, the great conservationist Gifford Pinchot might have failed in his efforts to save the upland forests of the region.

Episodes like this come to mind as I think of the time which Maurine and I have spent in politics generally and in the Legislature. I think of the conscientious, sincere newspaper reporter of liberal views who felt he had to apologize to us whenever the editorial page of his daily hammered our legislative bills. We finally told him that we had no abiding complaint so long as the news columns reported legislative occurrences without fear or favor.

I look back upon a letter I received from a chief of upper Columbia River Indians, when no other legislator would champion a resolution urging protection of their treaty fishing rights. 'You are a true ally of the red man,' said Yakima Charley. I could only wonder what my father's father, who had come from Germany in 1869 and banged away at Indians from a covered wagon, would have thought of that . . .

I shall always have great affection for the preacher of

Scotch ancestry with whom I worked in tandem on a petition to outlaw pari-mutuel gambling. 'Dick,' said he solemnly one afternoon, 'I spent all last night with my conscience debating if I should vote for you on election day. You are right on all the social and ethical questions but, by Heaven, you're an unreconstructed Democrat. I don't see how I can vote for a Democrat. I shall search my soul some more.'

Never did I discover how he marked his ballot, but I could only wish that all voting involved such painful and thorough introspection.

And I remember another minister, a tall Methodist in the orchard community of Hood River. Maurine and I had come there to do a story for *Saturday Review* about the efforts of a Legion commander to remove from the local Scroll of Honor the names of Nisei fruit growers who had fought with combat units of the United States Army in World War II. Some of the Nisei had been killed in action against the Nazis. Yet their names were threatened with elimination from the Honor Roll. The Methodist preacher had championed the Nisei during a period of hysteria. He had been threatened physically but had stood by the Nisei. We spent three days with him under these circumstances.

As the time came to leave Hood River, the Reverend Sherman Burgoyne stood in the doorway of his parish house. 'It's meant a lot to me to have folks in politics and writing come here to take my side,' he said. 'I kind of think people in town will be willing to help me now.'

Above the minister's head I could see the gleaming white glaciers of Mount Adams in the blue morning.

Their faces pass before me now—Oregon's people, scattered for 400 miles from the Pacific's tossing surf to the granite dome of Eagle Cap in the Wallowa Range. They are in quest of better government and a better way of life. Despite all the partisanship and crass motives and politicians' venality, they mean to gain their goals.

I can see the stalwart Negro athlete who felt that the civil rights law passed by the Legislature finally assured him the right to eat 'downstairs' in the dining rooms of hotels with his white teammates. He had tears of gratitude in his eyes. And I cannot forget the hard-boiled waitress, with two small children, who kissed Maurine's hand because the baby-sitting bill would let her deduct $60 a month before paying the state income tax.

Deeds such as this are trifling in the great scheme of human existence. But they are important in the daily lives of individual men, women and children. As long as politics can make such deeds possible, people of good will have to go into politics. It may be distasteful to them. It may expose them to abuse and criticism, even to that cruelest of all wounds, ridicule. Yet, still, they have to do it. Otherwise politics—and government—will be dominated by the element in our society which should not be entrusted with this responsibility and power.

If our political morality has failed to keep pace with progress in science and technology, then politics is the frontier where the most pioneering remains. Regardless of the odds, there must be people who can widen the trails through this trackless wilderness.

'When do I start, sir—and alone?' asked our great friend in the Mounted Police.

Appendix

—

POLITICS—AND YOU

ELIHU ROOT, who was a famous Secretary of State under Theodore Roosevelt and later a Senator from New York, said to some of his friends in 1920: 'Politics is the practical exercise of self-government, and somebody must attend to it if we are to have self-government. The principal ground of reproach against any American citizen should be that he is not a politician.'

What about you? There are at least 100,000 elective offices in the United States, ranging from the Presidency on down through legislatures and city councils, to constable or clerk in remote backwoods counties. Does your name fit one of these niches on the ballot?

Perhaps you are worried about your age, your religion, your physical appearance, a skeleton in the family closet, or about the limited time you spent in school and college. It could be that you have thought seriously of being a candidate for office in your state or local community and then abandoned the idea because of some handicap, real or imagined.

Indeed, you may even have asked yourself these specific questions, when you wondered whether you ever

could be chosen at the polls by your neighbors to speak
for them in the halls of government:

1. What Offices Can I Run For?

If you are an American citizen and old enough to
vote, nearly all public positions are legally within your
reach. A few call for a brief delay. To qualify for President of the United States, you must have been born in
this country and be 35 or older. A United States Senator must be 30 and have lived in this country nine years
or more. Many states require their Governors to be a
minimum of 30, and members of the Federal House of
Representatives must be at least 25 years of age.

Yet even these limitations occasionally are stretched.
In 1936 Rush D. Holt of West Virginia was elected to
the Senate when he was 29. The authorities decided that
his election had been valid if he would wait until his
30th birthday before formally presenting himself to take
the oath of office. But most elective posts within the
grasp of beginners exact only one basic requirement—
American citizenship.

2. Must I Belong to a Political Party?

From a practical standpoint, membership in either the
Republican or Democratic party is necessary if you are to
be elected to a seat in Congress, to the governorship of
your state, or to most legislatures. Yet many important
public positions, particularly in local areas, are 'nonpartisan.' This means that no party affiliation is needed. Of the
511 American cities with more than 25,000 inhabitants
each, 313 have nonpartisan elections. These communities
where you don't have to be a Republican or Democrat to
get into municipal office include such metropolises as San

Francisco, Milwaukee, Dallas, and Cincinnati. Furthermore, the legislatures of two states are chosen without regard to party labels—Nebraska and Minnesota.

However, you must face the fact that even nonpartisan
officials usually get their start in party ranks. Mayor
Norris Poulson of Los Angeles, for example, was elected
on a nonpartisan ballot but he became known by serving for nine years as a Republican member of Congress.

3. Do I Have to Belong to the Top Party in My State?

If you are a Republican in the South, your chances of
election to an important office are remote. Despite all the
fanfare and heraldry about the Eisenhower political revolution in the Southern states, its roots do not sink very
deep. The Republican Presidential slate carried Texas
by a safe margin in 1952, but the Texas legislature still
consists of 181 Democrats and no Republicans.

Similarly, there are many states above the Mason and
Dixon Line where a Democrat may be as forlorn as a
Republican in the South. Maine, Vermont, and Oregon
have not elected Democrats to the United States Senate
in modern times. Only two Democrats serve in the entire legislature of North Dakota and another two in the
sister state of South Dakota.

Yet occasionally this tide can be stemmed. Guy Gillette, a Democrat, sits in the United States Senate from
Republican Iowa. Maryland, once a Democratic strong-
hold, now has two Republican Senators. Remember these
exceptions when you make your own choice of parties.
Don't join a party merely because it is dominant in your
state. If you have violated your basic convictions, you
will be unhappy and inconsistent in politics. Your campaigning will lack sincerity. And, even in a minority

party, you can help bring pressure on the complacent majority to act in the public interest. As Democrats in Republican Oregon, my wife and I have seen this happen frequently on such important issues as modernizing the state constitution and preventing the despoliation of school lands.

4. *What If I Was Born in Another State?*

As Americans have continued to pilgrimage in vast numbers to new homes and jobs, the old argument has faded that only a 'native son' should prosper at the ballot box. Almost half of California's present population did not live in California ten years ago. One of the incumbent United States Senators from Oregon was born in Texas, the other in Wisconsin. Dwight D. Eisenhower ran for President as a resident of the state of New York, where he had lived for only a relatively short time.

Once the late Senator Charles Tobey of New Hampshire was taunted as a 'carpetbagger' because he had been born in Massachusetts. Tobey's reply was devastating: 'I selected the glorious state of New Hampshire through my own free choice. My opponent, having been born here, had no voice in the matter.'

5. *What If I Was Born in Another Country?*

This could be a more serious obstacle to political success. An unscrupulous adversary might use against you the fact that you had been an immigrant. Such an appeal to prejudice may take hold with some impressionable voters. Your best answer will be to cite American traditions. The authors of the Constitution of the United States provided that every public office except the Presidency could be filled by a naturalized citizen. There have been many illustrious examples of immigrants rising to political fame. Carl Schurz, Senator from Missouri and Secretary of the Interior, was born in Germany, and so was John Peter Altgeld, one of Illinois' bravest Governors. Scotland was the birthplace of William B. Wilson, the first man to serve as Secretary of Labor. Senator Robert F. Wagner of New York, pioneer sponsor of social security legislation, was another German immigrant. Charles A. Lindbergh, Sr., the flier's father and for many years a progressive Minnesota Congressman, voyaged to America from his native Sweden. Representative Steve Derounian of New York was born in Bulgaria.

6. *Will a Foreign Name Hurt My Chances?*

There can be no doubt that a name like 'Dinkelspiel' lacks the political lure of an Anglo-Saxon name with historic connotations, like 'Jackson' or 'Lewis.' Yet in some Congressional districts, where minorities are concentrated, a foreign-sounding name often has magic appeal. Michigan Congressmen are named Machrowicz and Lesinski, and Wisconsin is represented by a Zablocki and an O'Konski. It is said in Minnesota that a Scandinavian name is worth 100,000 votes and in Washington state at least 50,000 votes. The names of victorious candidates in these states tend to prove the thesis—Olson, Youngdahl, Andresen, Magnuson.

In other realms, a foreign name may not be so beneficial. Yet 'Eisenhower' is a name of undoubted Teutonic origin, and its owner lives at the White House. 'Hickenlooper' may provoke smiles, but it is the name of a man twice elected Senator from Iowa. 'Frelinghuysen' can tie tongues, and yet it appeared on franked envelopes as the signature of a famous New Jersey Senator.

In our own little sphere, my wife and I have not found the foreign-sounding name 'Neuberger' a detriment, although Oregon has only a relatively small population of German descent.

The late Senator Lewis B. Schwellenbach of Washington once said to me: 'It took quite a while to put across a name like "Schwellenbach," but it had one genuine advantage. People never forgot it. "Smith" or "Taylor" could slide right out of their minds, but not a name as awkward to pronounce and master as "Schwellenbach." '

7. Should I Change My Name?

If you take a new name completely, let a decent interval elapse before you run for public office. Voters will resent the fact that you may have changed your name merely to win their support. And don't shift to a new name unless the old one is positively ludicrous. This restraint, however, need not apply to superficial changes. Woodrow Wilson, for example, was born 'Thomas Woodrow Wilson.' And Champ Clark, a famous Speaker of the House of Representatives, shortened his name from 'James Beauchamp Clark.'

8. Does My Religion Make Any Difference?

Sad to relate, it probably does—in some places, at least. My state, where the Ku Klux Klan was powerful not so many years ago, has rarely elected a Catholic to high office. Prejudice against Catholics unquestionably weakened the Presidential chances of Alfred E. Smith in 1928. Yet there are encouraging signs that bigotry may be waning as a factor in elections. For the first time a Jew, Herbert H. Lehman of New York, has sat in the United States Senate by virtue of popular vote. One of the phenomenal feats of 1952 was performed by a Catholic, Mike Mansfield of Montana, who unseated an incumbent Republican Senator, even while General Eisenhower was sweeping that state for the Republican national ticket.

Under no circumstances, ever try to conceal your religion. If you are made the victim of intolerance, fight back and defy your foes. Never apologize or temporize in such a situation. When Lincoln was attacked as an infidel, he replied forthrightly, 'That I am not a member of any Christian Church is true. But I have never denied the truth of the Scriptures, and I have never spoken with intentional disrespect of religion in general, or of any denomination in particular . . . I do not think I could bring myself to support a man for office whom I knew to be an open enemy of, or scoffer at, religion.'

9. *What About My Age?*

If you are qualified by law to run for a tempting office, go ahead and put your name on the ballot. Rosalind Wiener, age 22, has recently been elected to the Los Angeles City Council. At the other end of life's spectrum, Theodore F. Green, age 86, is serving his third term as United States Senator from Rhode Island. Should the opposing side make an issue of either your youth or your alleged antiquity, you probably can rally most of the voters in that age bracket to your cause. Young people, however, are still in a decided minority in public life.

10. *Do I Have To Be a Talented Public Speaker?*

Naturally, a gift of gab never hurt anyone running for office—unless it seemed too slick and too much like that of a medicine-show barker. But you definitely don't have to be a dramatic orator who can shout in stentorian tones. Prime Minister Menzies of Australia once pointed out that public-address systems, with their helpful amplifiers, had diminished the value of old-style political oratory. President Eisenhower and ex-President Truman are examples of men who are not smooth or brilliant public speakers, but who have influenced voters by their plodding sincerity. Yet you must be able to articulate clearly so people will know what you are saying. If you require assistance in this respect, most of the colleges in your state are sure to have capable voice coaches.

11. *Do I Have To Be a War Veteran?*

Many Americans believe that a man who has served his country in war merits a special claim to preferment at the polls. General Eisenhower's brilliant career in the Army undoubtedly contributed to his political victory in 1952. According to the *Congressional Quarterly*, 61 out of the 96 members of the United States Senate are veterans of military service and 243 out of the 435 members of the House. Yet this does not mean you have to bow out if you are unable to call attention to service on the battlefield. Such successful vote-getters as President Franklin D. Roosevelt, Senator Robert A. Taft, and Governor Thomas E. Dewey never wore a uniform, either.

12. *Where Should I Start?*

The theory of crawling before you try to walk applies cogently to politics. Your local city council or state legislature are natural starting places, especially because you will be seeking votes only in the community where you are best known. School boards afford an able person a chance to show his mettle. You also might hanker to be county sheriff or district attorney. Do not be dazzled by the fact that such men as Arthur Vandenberg of Michigan, Wayne L. Morse of Oregon, and Stuart Symington of Missouri were elected United States Senators the first time they ever filed for office. Previous to this, you may be sure, they had acquired statewide and even national fame in fields like journalism, labor arbitration, and manufacturing.

13. *Should I Join a Lot of Fraternal Organizations?*

If you genuinely enjoy lodge work and the conviviality of fraternal fellowship, these contacts undoubtedly will help you at the polls. But better not to join at all than to use a lodge, callously and cynically, as merely a means of corralling votes. Your fraternal brothers are not fools. They will sense such opportunism and resent it bitterly.

14. *Do I Have To Be Supported by the Press?*

This may depend more upon the caliber of the newspapers than upon you. If the press in your community is fettered by partisanship and automatically endorses nearly all Republicans or all Democrats, as the case may be, then the attitude of these papers toward your candidacy will mean comparatively little. Indeed, some politicians have capitalized to advantage the mistrust of the press in their particular localities. On the other hand, truly independent newspapers like *The New York Times,* the *St. Louis Post-Dispatch,* the *Milwaukee Journal,* or the *Denver Post* can do much for a politician, because voters realize that such approval comes only after exhaustive editorial consideration of a candidate's qualifications.

15. *What If I Am Fat or Thin, Tall or Short?*

Don't be self-conscious about your appearance. If you are worried over the way you look, people will sense this shame and share it with you. Remember that American elections never have been an Atlantic City bathing-beauty contest. In *A Book About American Politics,* George Stimpson reports that President William Howarfd Taft weighed 354 pounds and President Grover Cleveland a rotund 250 pounds. Lincoln measured six feet four inches in height and George Washington six feet two. But Fiorello H. La Guardia, the most popular Mayor in the annals of New York City, was so short that his feet dangled a foot above the carpet when he sat at his desk. James Madison, twice elected President and the author of our Federal Constitution, weighed 100 pounds and stood a mere five feet four inches. He was ridiculed as 'Little Jemmy.' One newspaper, lampooning Lincoln's height in the election of 1864, twitted him as 'a long, lean, lank, lantern-jawed, high-cheeked-boned, spavined, rail-splitting stallion.'

16. *How Should I Dress When Campaigning?*

A shrewd member of the Senate once said, 'Don't dress up and don't dress down.' This is good advice, peren-

nially. I know a legislative candidate who deliberately
went to a meeting of Northwest sawmill workers in a
flannel shirt without a tie. He hoped to show them he
was 'one of the boys.' They were indignant and felt it
was a cheap stunt to win their votes. The more studied
and staged your attire, the greater likelihood it will be
the wrong thing to wear.

17. *What If I'm a Woman?*

Sheer mathematics prove that members of the female
sex confront an uphill struggle in American politics.
There are only eleven women in the U. S. House of
Representatives and but one, Margaret Chase Smith of
Maine, in the Senate. Women comprise a negligible 4
per cent of the 7,234 members of the 48 state legislatures. And yet women, for the first time in the history of
the United States, now outnumber men in the total population. This must mean that some lingering prejudice
exists against electing women to public office. For example, Dorothy McCullough Lee, who had done an outstanding job of cleaning up her city, was defeated for
re-election as Mayor of Portland, Oregon, by a candidate with the slogan of 'a man for a man's job.'

The woman who files for office must reconcile herself
to the fact that she will be tested more severely than
male candidates. Some of her most persistent critics are
likely to be members of her own sex, perhaps goaded
by jealousy. In general, she will have to be superior to
her male opponent in ideas, effort, and ease of expres-
sion, as my wife has discovered. Yet the isolated but
notable success of such women as Senator Smith, Congresswoman Edith Nourse Rogers of Massachusetts, ex-
Congresswoman Mary T. Norton of New Jersey, and

Mrs. Clare Boothe Luce should keep women trying to enter this field which so long has been dominated by men.

18. *Do I Have To Be a Precinct Worker or Party Official?*

Adlai E. Stevenson was elected Governor of Illinois on the Democratic ticket in 1948, although he never before had taken any part in Democratic party activities. One of the late Senator Vandenberg's biographers, Paul M. Cuncannon, has written of this man who served for 23 years as a Republican Senator from Michigan: 'The drudgery of practical politics did not appeal to him. He never busied himself with party organization. He was not a mixer with the county chairmen and with the boys who brought in the vote in the wards.'

The average candidate will not be able to remain so aloof, but he still can win an election without having been a doorbell-pusher or ward politician.

19. *What If I'm a Rich Man?*

If you have a lot of money, either through inheritance or business success, some demagogic adversary is sure to tell the electorate that you cannot possibly sympathize with the poor and the downtrodden. From then on, it's up to you. Franklin Roosevelt, Adlai Stevenson, and Robert A. Taft each endured such verbal assaults because of his family's wealth and made his own conduct an effective answer. Actually, if you possess the financial means to do so, you may have a patriotic duty to enter public life. Nelson A. Rockefeller, Under Secretary of Health and Welfare, has said: 'With the growing importance of government in our lives, as citizens we have the responsibility to participate to the extent that we can in local, county, state and national government. It's as simple as that.'

20. *What About Membership in a Labor Union?*

If you are a member in good faith of a legitimate trade union, it may help you at the polls. Most Americans glory in the fact that this country's political institutions permit a laboring man to rise to an important position in government. Many Congressional figures boast that they still 'hold a card' in a Railroad Brotherhood or the Butcher Workers. In fact, five former officials of leading trade unions now sit in the U. S. House of Representatives. Of course, there are some areas in the country where local hostility to unions exists. You will have to be the judge of this.

21. *Must I Be Married?*

Single people, of both sexes, have succeeded in American politics. A few observers believe that a dashing bachelor like Senator Warren Magnuson of the state of Washington has been helped at the polls by the linking of his name with those of movie starlets. Perhaps you must be as handsome as blond Senator Magnuson to have romantic conquests result in political advantage! There seems no doubt that a happy family life never hurt a candidate on election day.

22. *What If I Have Been Divorced?*

This is a far more complex question. Many people have strong religious and moral objections to divorce. They might be reluctant to vote for a man or woman whose marriage had failed. Yet this stern attitude could be relenting slightly, particularly where a divorce has not involved ugly notoriety or infidelity. Few political writers think that Adlai Stevenson's divorce was a factor in his defeat for the Presidency last year. Walter Kohler, Jr., was divorced in 1946 but he since has won two terms as Governor of Wisconsin. The amazing popularity of Franklin D. Roosevelt never seemed in peril because of the frequent divorces among his children.

23. What If I Have Been Mixed Up in a Scandal?

Once again, it all depends upon the circumstances. A sordid enough episode could finish off anybody for public office, yet, as beachwear gets skimpier, other mores appear to be relaxing too. Gossip and whispered slurs have lost some of their power to disturb us. The vilest innuendoes about the personal lives of FDR and General Eisenhower failed to tear down their reputations.

If you have been involved in an embarrassing situation and the facts are known, don't try to cover up. This will only make the situation seem worse. Voters can be tolerant of human frailties. In the campaign of 1884 Grover Cleveland was charged with fathering an illegitimate child. Cleveland immediately telegraphed his campaign manager: 'Whatever you say, tell the truth.' In defense of Cleveland, prominent clergymen pointed out that he had done the manly thing by supporting the child financially and giving it his name. Cleveland weathered the storm and was elected President. His counsel is still sound—'tell the truth.'

24. Suppose I Never Got to College?

Knowledge will help you to do a good job in office, and a college education usually means knowledge and erudition. But don't let the lack of college training give you an inferiority complex about filing for a political position. Thirteen Presidents of the United States never received a college degree, and these included Washington, Jackson, Lincoln, Cleveland, and Truman. The bulk of the people who pass upon your candidacy at the polls will be men and women whose own formal educations stopped at the end of high school or sooner.

25. *What Occupation Will Serve Me Best?*

Lawyers dominate our public life. This may be because legislation and laws are related so intimately to the work of the legal profession. Furthermore, lawyers ordinarily are skilled in self-expression. The *Congressional Quarterly* has revealed that 'well over half the Senate and the House represent former lawyers or judges.' Businessmen and bankers follow next in order, comprising roughly one-third of Congress. Farmers are third in line, with 21 Senators and 63 Representatives from the ranks of agriculture.

Yet this need not discourage you if you are a butcher, baker, or physician. Nearly all professions and specialties are represented somewhere in American public life. The popular sheriff of our county is an ex-fireman. One of our most capable State Senators manages a restaurant association, another is a radio announcer. A former nightclub band leader served for 20 years as Washington's Lieutenant-Governor. Eskimo and Indian fishermen sit today in the Alaskan Territorial legislature at Juneau. And some candidates in Oregon even have been triumphant by capitalizing on irritation over the attorneys' monopoly. They placed on the ballot the sly but crude slogan, 'Not a lawyer'!

26. *Will Being an Intellectual Handicap Me?*

This is another situation in which it is entirely up
to the pluck and resourcefulness of the person under
criticism. A wave of anti-intellectual sentiment has
gripped some people. Men have been ridiculed because
they seem scholarly. Yet the author of the Declaration
of Independence, Thomas Jefferson, took pride in being
an intellectual and so did the 28th President, Woodrow
Wilson. In 1936 Senator William E. Borah of Idaho
told me as we drove through the Snake River Valley,
'Every unfair charge in a political campaign can be
made to react against its originators—if it is thrown back
quickly and courageously.'

27. *Will I Have To Compromise My Principles?*

All of us are familiar with the candidates who cry out
for a firm stand against Soviet Russia but advise mothers their sons shouldn't have to be drafted into the
Army. Unfortunately, these candidates are not always
defeated. Only a Pollyanna would claim that political
double talk never pays off. You will be tempted to tell
each group exactly what it hopes to hear. In politics you
will meet many men who demand tax reduction in one
breath but constantly seek more pork-barrel spending
for their own home districts. It will be a personal decision whether you want to follow this course.

It has been our personal experience that the conscientious citizen in politics usually makes a mistake when
he backs down on basic principles.

Mrs. Neuberger and I were sponsoring a bill to require full disclosure of the funds spent campaigning for
public office. Opponents of the bill persuaded us, against

our better judgment, to agree to modifications which
greatly diluted the proposal. All at once, we discovered
that the changes had destroyed the enthusiasm of civic-
reform groups which had been whole-heartedly behind
us. With this support weakened, the bill died in the
State Senate. Too late, we realized we would have been
infinitely better off had we stuck to the original bill,
which actually expressed our true principles.

If you enter public life, you will have to decide
when a compromise threatens your ideals and when it
simply blends your own views with those of some other
honest person. Two comments by President Lincoln
illustrate the difference. 'Compromises of principle
break down of their own weight,' said he. Yet Lincoln
also declared: 'The spirit of compromise and mutual
concession first gave us the Constitution.'

28. *Is Honesty the Best Policy in Politics?*

You can be honest without shouting to the housetops
all ideas which run counter to local pride and foibles. It
is true that Senator George W. Norris of Nebraska
once boldly defied a vast throng that was belligerent because he had voted against America's entrance into
World War I. But only a man of special capacity can
challenge the popular will so spectacularly. You need
not feel you are deceitful if you keep to yourself some
controversial political notion. Theodore Roosevelt in-
sisted that it was the task of the leader to think what the
people think, but to think it first. By this he meant no
politician should separate himself completely from public opinion.

Because he deliberately muted his views on the archaic seniority system, the late Senator Robert M. La Follette, Jr., was able to achieve some streamlining of Congressional procedure. Had he spoken too bluntly about the question of seniority, all the elderly members of the Senate and House would have been antognized. As a consequence, no reforms whatsoever could ever have resulted.

My wife and I are Democrats in a legislature that is one-sidedly Republican. For this reason, although we have been championing civil rights for many years, we purposely put our own names near the end on Oregon's civil rights bill. We encouraged Republican legislators to lead off, because we realized that conspicuous sponsorship by the small Democratic minority might have jeopardized the bill's chances.

Professor Hugh A. Bone of the University of Washington, who is the author of *American Politics and the Party System,* has pointed out that participation in partisan politics frequently calls for diplomacy and self-discipline. Party platforms are long and involved. If each Republican or Democrat spoke up whenever he could not go along with every advocacy of his party, the parties might collapse completely and no unified effort would be possible.

Senator Robert Taft swallowed his pride and, in the interest of party harmony, promoted the program on Capitol Hill of a President who had defeated him for the Republican nomination. Unless such personal concessions often took place, politics in the United States would be reduced to unending personal strife and bickering. Truculence, after all, is not a synonym for courage. You must learn to distinguish between surrender and mere conciliation.

29. *Will I Need a Lot of Money?*

If you are running for a comparatively minor office, you might get by with a campaign fund of a few hundred dollars. But candidates for the U. S. Senate in even sparsely settled states like Oregon now have campaign exchequers exceeding $75,000. In populous Pennsylvania, these funds may reach $750,000. Two reasons account for such enormous spending: (1) the flabby weakness of laws designed to control campaign expenses, and (2) the desire of selfish special interests to have important public officials in their debt.

As we have seen in this book, the question of campaign expenditures is one of the thorniest problems confronting American democracy.

30. *Where Will I Get the Money for My Campaign Fund?*

This will be one of the principal tests of your integrity. Many special interests hope to have public officials in their debt. One way is to donate lavishly to political campaign funds. Money may be offered you by the underworld, by people who want to loot public timber lands, by men anxious to sidestep competitive bidding on state or county contracts.

Railroads, banks, private utilities, dairies, trade unions, auto dealers, doctors, lumbermen—these are all special interests of one sort or another. They want certain kinds of legislation passed or defeated.

What rule should you follow in accepting donations from such sources? We know of but one precept which will lead to real contentment in public life. It is this— allow yourself to be obligated for financial support only to groups with which you are in fundamental harmony. Never become tethered by checks or cash to interests whose program you believe to be ethically wrong.

For example, if you think organized labor is generally heading in the right direction, you have no reason to reproach yourself for accepting a contribution from a union. If you have faith that the doctors in your state are promoting the public welfare, you will not be guilty of inconsistency if you let the local medical society pay for your campaign brochures. You must get financial help from somewhere under our present system of wide-open political spending. Obtain this help from sources you regard as worthy.

Two other rules should be heeded: (1) Rely on issues rather than money to defeat your adversary, for that is the American way, and (2) never become indebted financially to a person who might expect some illegal favor in return for his beneficence.

31. *What About My Health?*

It would be a good idea to have a thorough medical checkup before putting your name on the ballot. Campaigning for public office wears down a person, both physically and spiritually. You will have to absorb a lot of unfair abuse and yet never show temper or outrage. Frequently you will be buttonholing voters and giving speeches from dawn until midnight. If you suffer from a serious and persistent organic ailment, you should consider carefully before entering the maelstrom of active politics.

On the other hand, do not be deterred by the fact that you may be crippled. Congressman Joseph J. Mansfield of Texas served for many years in a wheelchair.

Senator Charles E. Potter of Michigan is a legless veteran of World War II. Franklin Roosevelt could move
about only with steel braces and the assistance of heavy
canes. 'I'm President with my head, not with my legs,'
he once told a visitor to the White House.

32. *What Is the Best Way To Campaign?*

If you have a bulging campaign treasury, you can
spend it on billboards, newspaper advertising, direct-mail
solicitation, and TV and radio time. Limited finances
must be husbanded more carefully. A greater burden is
on the candidate himself. He must meet the voters face
to face—in their homes and stores, during lunch hours
at factories and logging camps, at public meetings and
picnics, even on street corners where people congregate
while waiting for busses and trolleys.

33. *Should I Be My Own Boss?*

In politics, everyone offers advice. Methods for winning elections are volunteered as freely as remedies for
the common cold. But in the final analysis, you must
make fundamental decisions yourself. Your own stake in
the outcome exceeds that of all others. You cannot even
let your family push you around, either before or after
getting into office. One of the great letters of American
politics is that which President Wilson pecked out himself on a portable typewriter, refusing his own brother
Joseph the postmastership at Nashville, Tennessee.

34. *Will 'Witch-Hunting' Win Me Votes?*

Dark currents run in many men. Somewhere, prejudices may lurk against Negroes or American Indians or
other minorities. There may be voters who harbor long-

smoldering resentments against schoolteachers, priests, rabbis, foreigners, bankers, or migratory agricultural workers. Perhaps you can collect some unthinking votes by stirring hysteria against these people. Yet, if you are a normal American citizen, with a nagging conscience, no public office gained by such methods is likely to bring you satisfaction or personal happiness.

35. *Should I Try Again If I Lose the First Time?*

You will be a poor American if one political licking retires you permanently from public life. Lincoln was defeated by Stephen A. Douglas for the United States Senate in 1858, but two years later attained the Presidency and lasting fame. FDR lost overwhelmingly as a candidate for Vice President in 1920, but lived to see himself elected four times to the White House. Even after his stunning 1948 defeat for President, Thomas E. Dewey rallied to win a third term in 1950 as Governor of the nation's largest state, New York. Both William Howard Taft and Charles Evans Hughes suffered crushing Presidential defeats at the ballot box, but went on to achieve eminence as Chief Justices of the United States Supreme Court.

Rare, indeed, is the prominent figure in American public life who has not absorbed his share of reversals in political contests. I knew a distinguished Oregon resident who was beaten for a seat on the State Supreme Court by the excruciating margin of 34,609 votes to 34,608. He said:

'The world had fallen in on me. I was tormented by the knowledge that I would have won if only I had shaken several more hands, if I had gone to the pioneers' picnic which I had missed because of a headache, if I had taken time to write a couple of additional letters to acquaintances. I was about to withdraw from public life completely, when I began to think that these reasons made it all the more imperative that I keep on trying. If such trivial things could explain my defeat, the next time I surely would win.'

This man was Charles L. McNary. He later served for twenty-seven years in the United States Senate, was Republican floor leader for more than a decade, and today one of the great Federal hydroelectric dams across the Columbia River is named in his honor.

INDEX

Index prepared by Maurine Neuberger